KEYBOA
& COMPUTER
MUSIC

Philip Hawthorn

Consultants: Vince Hill and Peter Howell

Designed by Kim Blundell

CW00866997

Edited by Judy Tatchell
Computer program written by Chris Oxlade
Music written by Philip Hawthorn

Illustrated by Michael Gilbert, Kim Blundell,
Martin Newton, Brenda Haw, Stuart Trotter,
Adam Willis, Peter Bull, Roger Stewart
and Chris Lyon

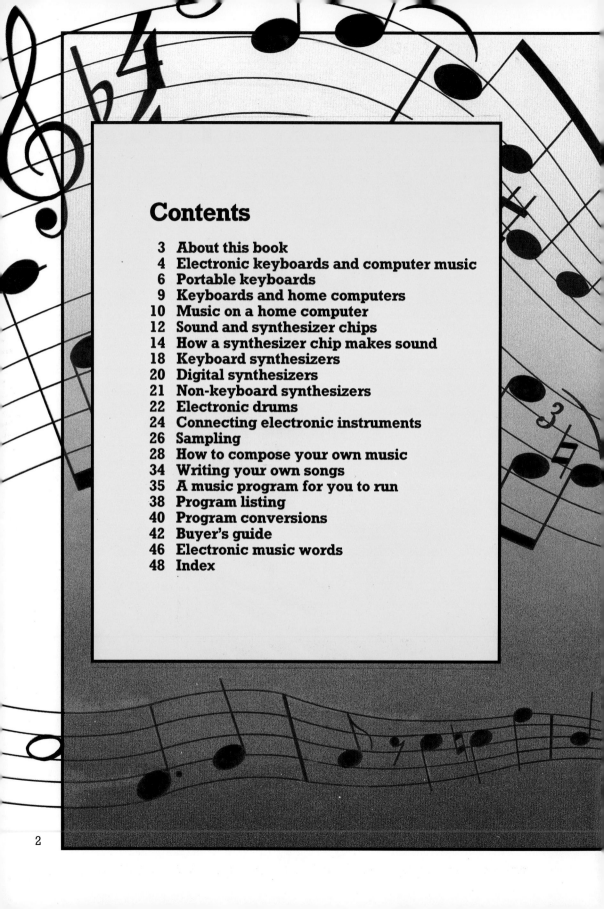

Contents

About this book

This book is about electronic music and the instruments that make it. These range from cheap portable keyboards, which you can use at home, to large expensive synthesizers which you see being played by pop groups and bands.

You will see other electronic instruments as well, such as drums and guitars. You can find out how all these instruments are played and how they make the music you hear on records.

The book also includes the most sophisticated electronic music instruments in the world. These can play music with any sound you can think of, and also make sounds which no one has ever heard before.

Later on in the book you can find out how to compose your own music and write your own songs. This means looking at tunes, rhythms, bass and harmonies as well as words (called lyrics). This section also has a specially written song with instructions on how you can play it.

If you have a home computer, you can find out how to use it to play and store music. The extra things you can buy to help you, such as programs and equipment to plug in, are described as well.

There is an exciting music program on page 38 for you to type into your computer* which lets you compose and play tunes. Depending on your computer, you can use any of five different sounds, add a rhythm and also store your tunes.

At the end of the book is a Buyer's Guide to help you if you want to buy an electronic keyboard, music programs or extra music equipment for your computer.

3

*The program will run on the Commodore 64, BBC, Spectrum, Electron, VIC 20 and MSX.

Electronic keyboards and computer music

Almost every pop group or band nowadays uses electronic keyboards in concerts and on their records. These keyboards can make sounds that ordinary instruments could never do. They can also make the sound of nearly any musical instrument you can think of, so you may not even realize that you are listening to electronic music.

On these two pages you can see some different keyboards and other electronic instruments which appear later in the book. You can also find out where you might hear electronic music.

Electronic instruments

In this picture there are some electronic instruments you may recognize from watching pop groups on television.

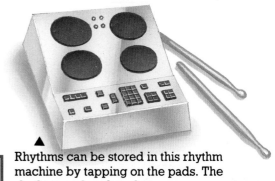

▲

Rhythms can be stored in this rhythm machine by tapping on the pads. The rhythm can be played back to accompany a song.

More about electronic keyboards

There are many types of electronic keyboard. You may see them in music shops and also in shops that stock computer equipment. This is because each one has a built-in computer.

Speakers

This is a portable (or home) keyboard. It is quite cheap. It has built-in speakers. It lets you choose between a number of different types of sound and automatic rhythms. You can find out more about this type of keyboard over the page.

▲

This is called an electronic keyboard or synthesizer. Just the one keyboard can make lots of different sounds.

Electronic instruments can be linked together so that one of them can control all the others.

Some keyboards can be played like this. On the handle are controls which affect notes while they are sounding, e.g. make them rise or fall.

You can find out about linking electronic instruments on pages 24-25.

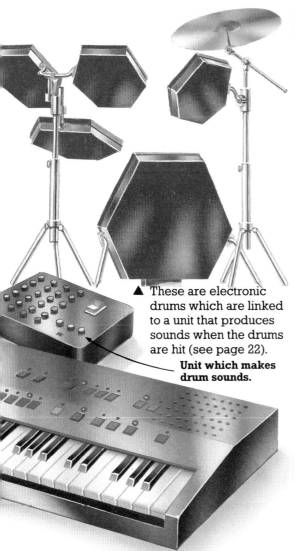

▲ These are electronic drums which are linked to a unit that produces sounds when the drums are hit (see page 22).

Unit which makes drum sounds.

Home computer music

Many home computers are capable of making, playing and storing music to play back later. You can buy music programs and extra music equipment for most computers. This makes it easier to write and play music. There is more about home computer music on pages 9-11.

Television

Some television stations have their own electronic music and sound workshops. Here they record music and sound effects for many of the programmes and videos you watch. The workshops contain some of the most sophisticated and expensive electronic equipment. You can see some of this on page 27.

The music business

Electronic keyboards can make such exciting music that they have revolutionized the record industry. Music can be composed and played on them and other electronic equipment used to record it.

The latest electronic recording equipment is used to record this compact disc. This means that you do not hear any background noise when it is played.

Have a look on your record sleeves to see if you can find the names of any electronic keyboards, such as the Fairlight or Synclavier.*

5

More about these on page 27.

Portable keyboards

You can buy portable keyboards for a lot less than a home computer. They are also called home or single keyboards. They can be plugged into the mains or run on batteries, depending on the keyboard.

You can play music on a portable keyboard even if you cannot play any other musical instruments. Using only one or two fingers, you can build up quite complex music. You can play tunes you know or make up new ones.

On the next three pages you can find out about the different types of portable keyboard and the things you can do on them.

Music memory

Music from keyboard's memory.

Music you play "live".

Preset rhythms

Some portable keyboards let you store your own music in their memories. You can then play back the stored music and play another part "live" on the keyboard along with it. Some keyboards have two memories, so you can store two parts and play them back at once.

Keyboard sizes

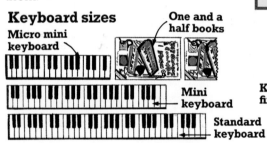

Micro mini keyboard

One and a half books

Mini keyboard

Standard keyboard

The smallest portable keyboards are called micro mini keyboards. They are about one and a half times the length of this book. There are also larger ones called mini and standard keyboards. Generally, the larger the keyboard, the more you can do with it. The picture on the right shows a standard keyboard.

The transposer dial makes everything you play on the keyboard higher or lower. This is so that you can play in tune with other instruments.

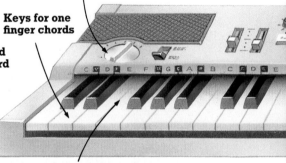

Keys for one finger chords

This standard keyboard has 61 keys. Micro mini keyboards have about 30 keys.

Different sounds

You can choose from up to 20 different kinds of sound to play your tunes, ranging from musical instruments to weird electronic noises. These sounds are called presets. There are a number of buttons on the keyboard which you press to select a preset.

Different rhythms

The keyboard also has rhythms, such as disco or rhumba, which you can use to accompany your tunes. Most keyboards give you a choice of between four and 20 rhythms. You can set the speed and the volume of the rhythm and also make it start automatically when you begin playing.

Automatic accompaniments

Portable keyboards have several automatic accompaniments which you can use with your tunes. For example, the keyboard can add a bass line. This consists of low notes which match your tune. You can control both its volume and speed.

A chord is more than one note at once.

An arpeggio is the notes in a chord played one after the other.

You can find out lots more about music on page 28.

Most portable keyboards have a switch, sometimes labelled "Autochord". If this is on, the keyboard will automatically add two more notes to any one you play at the lower end of the keyboard. These three notes are called a chord.

The keyboard can play the notes that make up a chord one after the other. These are called arpeggios. The button which you press to obtain this effect is often labelled the "Arpeggiator".

Socket for headphones so you can practise without anyone else hearing.

This keyboard has stereo speakers. Sometimes they are mounted on to keyboards instead of being built in.

The keyboard can be connected to the amplifier in a hi-fi system, to improve the sound or to record what you play.

Rhythm buttons

A foot pedal can be attached to the keyboard to control the volume, leaving both hands free for playing.

Accompaniment buttons

Manual rhythm keys

Manual rhythms

Some keyboards allow you to record your own rhythms. You press a button which makes the keys at the top of the keyboard produce the sound of rhythm instruments, such as drums.

Single and multiple notes

Most micro mini keyboards only allow you to play one note at a time. This is called monophony. You can still add stored chords and rhythms, though. Larger keyboards let you play up to eight notes at once. Playing more than one note at a time is called polyphony.

In the picture you can see two lines of music. The top line is monophonic, the bottom line, polyphonic.

Playcard keyboard

This type of portable keyboard has all the functions described on the previous two pages. It can also play music pre-recorded on to special cards, called playcards.

All the information for one piece of music is stored electronically on a strip at the bottom of the card. You can run the card along the groove in the keyboard to feed the information in.

Once the music is stored in the keyboard's memory you can do different things with it, as described below.

Tune is written out on top portion of card.

Card slides along groove to store music in keyboard's memory.

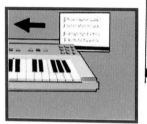

Strip stores tune (or melody), harmony, bass, rhythm and chords.

Playcard controls

Chord display window

Chord lamps

Melody lamps

Autoplay: Plays the music back with all the parts.

Lamp cancel: Allows you to play the melody by yourself without the lamps coming on.

Free tempo: Makes the accompaniment go at the same speed as you play the melody.

Chord cancel: Plays back all the music except the chords. You can play them yourself by following the lamps over the keys. The name of the chord is displayed in the chord display window.

Melody cancel: Plays back all the music except the melody. You can play this yourself on the keyboard. Small lamps above the keys light up to show you which notes to play.

Groove for playcard

Phrase repeat: Helps you learn to play the music a few notes (called a phrase) at a time. You repeat them until you can play them correctly.

Chord learn: Makes the keyboard wait for you to play the right chord before continuing the music.

Printed music

Printer built into keyboard.

Printing keyboard

This type of portable keyboard can print out music which you have just played or stored in the keyboard's memory. This enables you to make up a tune and then get a copy of it in musical notation.

Keyboards and home computers

If you have a home computer, you may be able to buy a keyboard to plug into it. Together, they will do the same kinds of things as a portable keyboard.

You cannot play music on this type of keyboard by itself. It needs the part of a computer which makes sound to make it work, called the synthesizer chip.

The keyboard comes with programs, or software, for the computer. Some software, called synthesis software, enables the computer to make different types of sound. Other software, called sequencing software, lets you store tunes. Some software lets you do both.

Connecting keyboards

Software produces graphics on the screen.

Music program on cassette or disk.

Keyboard connects to expansion port.

You can connect some portable keyboards to computers. More about this on page 25.

The keyboard usually connects to the expansion port on the computer. Before you can operate it you must load the software into the computer.

Synthesis software

Synthesis software usually lets you choose from a number of stored sounds (or presets). These are shown on the screen.

M means monophonic presets (you can only play one note at a time).

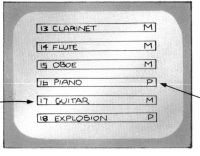

13 CLARINET	M
14 FLUTE	M
15 OBOE	M
16 PIANO	P
17 GUITAR	M
18 EXPLOSION	P

You may be able to create your own sounds, too. You can find out more about this on pages 14-17.

P means polyphonic presets (you can play up to three notes at a time).

Sequencing software

The computer stores the notes of a tune as you play them on the keyboard. You can then use the computer keys to alter them, change the speed (or tempo) and select different presets if the software allows you to.

Sequencing software shows you the tune on the screen as you enter it. There are two types of sequencing: real time and step time.

Sequencing in real time

Yeah

In real time, you play "live" and the computer remembers the tune. Some software then allows you to alter, or edit, the tune if you have not played it correctly.

Sequencing in step time

Keyboard tells computer how high or low the note is.

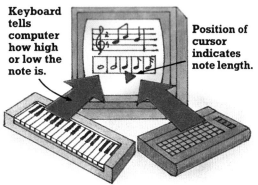

Position of cursor indicates note length.

In step time, you give the computer your tune one note at a time. You tell the computer how long you want each note to be, and then play it on the keyboard. You can use step time sequencing to store music too difficult to play at the proper speed.

Music on a home computer

If you have a home computer, you may be able to buy software for it which lets you play and write music without using one of the keyboards shown on the previous page.

As well as buying ready-written programs on tape or disk, there are sometimes music programs for you to copy in magazines or books. There is a music program to try on page 38.

You can also buy extra equipment, or hardware, which enables you to make better music on your computer. Some of this is shown on the opposite page.

> You can play your computer like a musical instrument.

Playing music on your computer

You can play music on your computer like you would on a musical instrument, by using synthesis software (see page 9). You play notes by pressing the computer keys. The manual supplied with the software tells you which key to press for which note.

There are usually a number of stored sounds (presets) to choose from, ranging from musical instruments to sound effects like a train or an explosion.

Composing and storing music on your computer

Sequencing software lets you compose and store tunes on your computer. Some software lets you write music with more than one part, and also to add stored rhythms.

Once you have stored the music inside the computer, most software lets you alter, or edit it. You can insert, change or delete notes. When you have finished writing your tune, you can store it on tape or disk.

You enter the notes from the keyboard, usually in step time, i.e. one note at a time. You do this in one of the two ways described below, depending on the software.

1. Typing in music

Part

Preset rhythm

Length

Name of note

Octave

PART: 1   RHYTHM: 2

1. C-2. 1
2. F-1. 1
3. G-1. 1/2
4. A-1. 1/2

Note number (first note in tune = 1 etc.).

With this kind of software, you type in the musical name of the note, e.g. C# (pronounced "C sharp"), and its length.

You also have to give another piece of information, called the octave. The notes on a keyboard are divided up into sections called octaves. You usually get a range of three octaves to use, so you have to say which number octave the note you want is in.

2. Using the cursor

Stave with musical notes.

Note lengths

Cursor showing where next note will go.

The screen display gives you a picture of a musical line, called a stave. You select each note by placing the cursor on the line or space where you want the note to go.*

You can specify its length either by typing it on the keyboard (e.g. "1" for one beat), or from a menu on the screen, which shows you the different note lengths.

To move the cursor you usually use the cursor control keys. Some software allows you to use a joystick instead.

Joystick   Cursor control keys

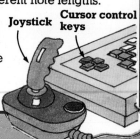

10

*There is more about this in the music-writing section starting on page 28.

Extra music equipment

On this page you can see some of the extra equipment you can buy to help you use your computer to make music.

Keyboard overlays

Keyboard overlay

Some software comes with a keyboard overlay, which resembles a piano keyboard. It fits over your computer keyboard. When you press a key on the overlay, it activates a computer key. It is easier to play than a computer keyboard.

Sound boxes

To computer

You can buy a sound box to connect to your computer. This is quite expensive. It contains a more complex synthesizer chip** than the one in the computer. It gives you more presets and extra memory space to store music.

Printing music

Most software lets you print out music which you have stored, using a printer. This enables you to write music and then give it to someone to play on a musical instrument.

Loudspeakers

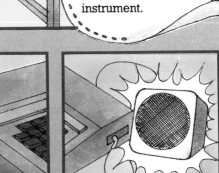

Built-in speaker

Many computers use the loudspeaker on the television to which they are connected to produce sound . . .

. . . Others have their own built-in speaker.

You can buy an add-on loudspeaker for some computers which improves their sound quality.

Hi-fi amplifier

Audio/Video socket

Some computers allow you to play the sound through a hi-fi system. You use a lead which connects the Audio/Video socket on the computer to the Auxiliary socket on the amplifier.

**The part of a computer which makes sound.

Sound and synthesizer chips

In the rest of this book you will find out more about how to play and write electronic music. To enable you to do this better, you need to know how synthesizer chips store and produce sounds. Most instruments have their own individual sound. The preset sounds on an electronic keyboard imitate these sounds. Here you can find out how.

How loud or soft it is (i.e. its volume).

How high or low it is (called the pitch).

The quality of the sound, called the timbre (e.g. a flute and a trombone playing the same note sound very different).

What is sound?

A sound is made when something vibrates, or oscillates, e.g. when you pluck a rubber band. There are three things you can say to describe a sound, shown in the picture above.

Sound travels through air because a vibrating object makes the air particles next to it vibrate. These bump into other particles and repeatedly squash together and separate again. You can draw a graph which represents this, as shown on the right. Graphs like this are sometimes referred to as sound waves.

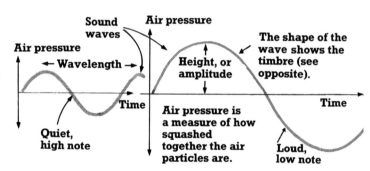

Sound waves

Air pressure

Air pressure

← Wavelength →

Height, or amplitude

The shape of the wave shows the timbre (see opposite).

Time

Quiet, high note

Air pressure is a measure of how squashed together the air particles are.

Time

Loud, low note

Loudness

The loudness, or volume, is indicated by the height, or amplitude, of the wave. The higher the wave, the louder the sound.

Pitch

The pitch of a note depends on the wavelength of the wave, i.e. the distance between two peaks. The shorter the wavelength the higher the note.

Frequency

One wavelength represents ▶ one oscillation, or vibration, of the wave.

◀ The number of oscillations a sound wave makes in one second is called the frequency.

The shorter the wavelength, the higher the frequency. High frequencies represent high notes. Frequency is measured in Hertz.

High frequency

Low frequency

Hertz is written Hz.

Musical notes

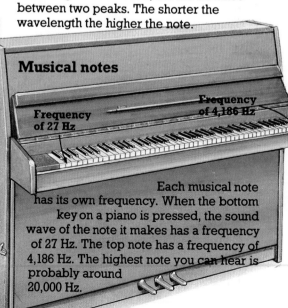

Frequency of 27 Hz

Frequency of 4,186 Hz

Each musical note has its own frequency. When the bottom key on a piano is pressed, the sound wave of the note it makes has a frequency of 27 Hz. The top note has a frequency of 4,186 Hz. The highest note you can hear is probably around 20,000 Hz.

Timbre

The timbre depends on the actual shape of the sound wave. Here are the basic waves that are stored in a synthesizer chip. It can combine or change these to make other sounds.

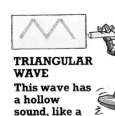

TRIANGULAR WAVE
This wave has a hollow sound, like a flute.

SAWTOOTH WAVE
A sawtooth wave has a harsh sound, like a brass instrument.

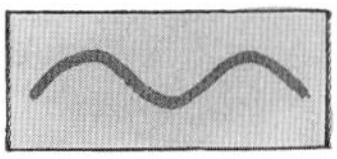

SINE WAVE
A sine wave represents the purest sound. It is the simplest wave.

SQUARE WAVE
This has a reedy sound, like a mouth organ or accordion.

WHITE NOISE
This noise is like the hiss that you hear when your radio is not tuned in properly.

Storing sound electronically

A synthesizer chip stores a sound as a set of numbers describing the sound wave. The numbers represent the height of the wave at frequent intervals. You can see this in the picture. The process of converting a wave into numbers is called digitization.

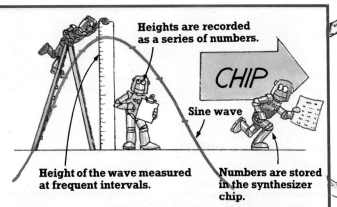

Heights are recorded as a series of numbers.

CHIP

Sine wave

Height of the wave measured at frequent intervals.

Numbers are stored in the synthesizer chip.

What makes sounds different from each other

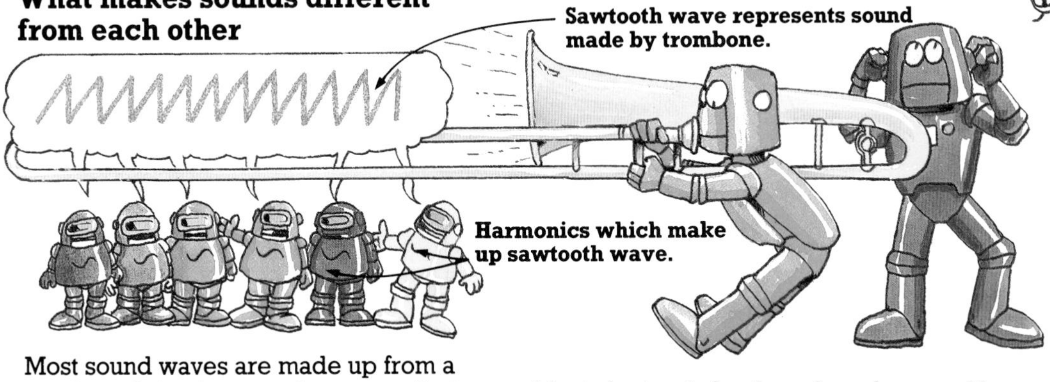

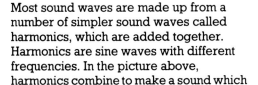

Sawtooth wave represents sound made by trombone.

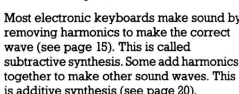

Harmonics which make up sawtooth wave.

Most sound waves are made up from a number of simpler sound waves called harmonics, which are added together. Harmonics are sine waves with different frequencies. In the picture above, harmonics combine to make a sound which is represented by a sawtooth wave.

Most electronic keyboards make sound by removing harmonics to make the correct wave (see page 15). This is called subtractive synthesis. Some add harmonics together to make other sound waves. This is additive synthesis (see page 20).

13

How a synthesizer chip makes sound

The synthesizer chip inside a keyboard or computer is like a factory for making sounds. It has lots of different departments. The main ones deal with pitch, timbre and volume. The workers in each department can make a large variety of sounds.

As well as using preset (stored) sounds, most home computers with synthesis software enable you to make your own. You do this by adjusting the controls, or parameters, which the software displays on the screen (see the picture on the right).

Portable keyboards have a number of preset sounds which cannot be changed. Larger keyboards (like the one on page 18) allow you to change presets to make your own sounds.

On the next four pages you can find out all about the sound factory.

Software screen display

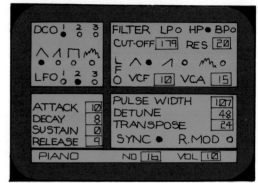

An example of the screen display of a piano preset.

The picture above shows the type of screen display provided by most synthesis software. Each part of the sound-making process is shown. They are all explained on the next four pages. You change the settings in each department using the cursor control keys.

OSCILLATOR DEPARTMENT

Pitch

The Oscillator Department deals with the pitch. When you press a key on the keyboard, a signal is sent to the part that makes the sound, called the oscillator. This signal tells the oscillator the pitch of the note you want played.

You can set the oscillator to produce a sound with any of the basic waves (see previous page).

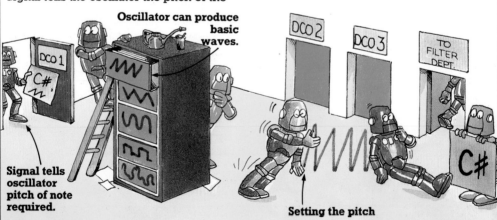

Oscillator can produce basic waves.

Signal tells oscillator pitch of note required.

Setting the pitch

There are two kinds of oscillator: a Voltage Controlled Oscillator (VCO) and a Digital Controlled Oscillator (DCO). They both do the same thing, but a DCO is more accurate. Most synthesizer chips use DCOs.

In the picture, the sound is shown as a wave. In the chip, however, the sound is stored and processed as a set of numbers (i.e. digitally). You do not actually hear the sound until it comes out of the speaker.

Many synthesizer chips have more than one oscillator. You can use each oscillator to play a different note. You can also use all the oscillators to play the same note at once.

Timbre

The type of sound, or timbre, is changed by a filter. When the wave arrives at the filter it is made up of lots of harmonics. The filter only lets some of them through. This changes the shape of the wave, and therefore the timbre. The filter is called a Voltage Controlled Filter, or VCF.

Each harmonic has a different frequency (number of oscillations per second). You can set a "cut-off" frequency that determines which harmonics are allowed to go through. Those that are not allowed to go through are cut off, or attenuated. This is subtractive synthesis (see previous page).

You set the cut-off frequency using the cursor controls. The effect of the cut-off on the sound depends on the type of filter (see below).

Filters

A low pass filter only allows the frequencies below the cut-off point to pass. It gives a mellow sound for woodwind and brass.

A high pass filter allows only those above the cut-off point to pass. It makes a tinny sound used for strings.

A band pass filter allows a band of frequencies either side of the cut-off point to pass. This is used for piano or guitar sounds.

More filter controls

Resonating harmonics

You can change the timbre even further by using resonance. This makes a ringing sound. Resonance increases the amplitude, or height, of the harmonic waves around the cut-off point. The higher the setting, the more harmonics are affected and the more resonance there is.

When most instruments play a note, the timbre changes while the note is sounding. Imagine the sound of a gong, for instance. Computers and keyboards have a control called the envelope generator (EG) which can vary the timbre as the note is playing. It shapes the waves as they pass through the filters.

Volume

The volume of the sound in a synthesizer factory is determined by the Voltage Controlled Amplifier, or VCA.

When you hear a note played on, say, a piano, the volume changes as the note sounds. You can vary the volume of the note you play on your keyboard to make it sound more realistic.

The part that does this is the volume envelope generator or EG, (not to be confused with the filter EG described on the previous page).

What the volume envelope generator does

The volume envelope generator works by shaping the wave as it passes through the VCA. It does this in four stages called Attack, Decay, Sustain and Release.

Attack: how quickly note sounds i.e. how long it takes to reach full volume.

Decay: how quickly note dies away after reaching full volume.

Sustain: volume level of note whilst key is being pressed.

Release: how quickly note dies away after key is released.

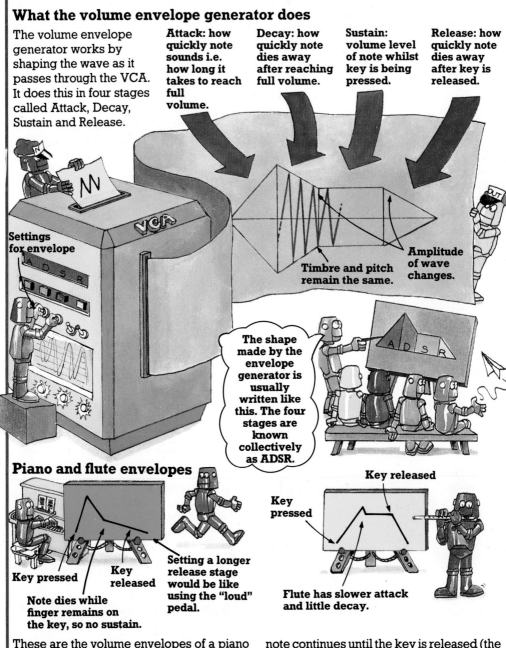

Settings for envelope

A D S R

Timbre and pitch remain the same.

Amplitude of wave changes.

The shape made by the envelope generator is usually written like this. The four stages are known collectively as ADSR.

Piano and flute envelopes

Key pressed

Key released

Setting a longer release stage would be like using the "loud" pedal.

Note dies while finger remains on the key, so no sustain.

Key pressed

Key released

Flute has slower attack and little decay.

These are the volume envelopes of a piano and a flute preset. If you keep your finger on the key, the piano note dies away slowly because there is no sustain stage. The flute note continues until the key is released (the equivalent of when a flute player stops blowing).

More ways to vary the timbre

If your keyboard or computer has more than one oscillator, you can use the wave from one to affect that of another. This is called modulation. It is rather like having two colours and mixing them together to make a new one. There are several ways in which you can modulate sound, as you can see below.

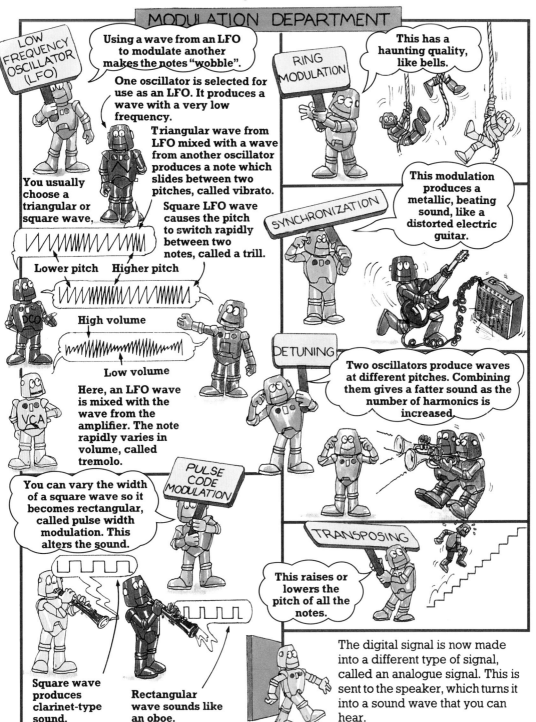

MODULATION DEPARTMENT

LOW FREQUENCY OSCILLATOR (LFO)

Using a wave from an LFO to modulate another makes the notes "wobble".

One oscillator is selected for use as an LFO. It produces a wave with a very low frequency.

Triangular wave from LFO mixed with a wave from another oscillator produces a note which slides between two pitches, called vibrato.

You usually choose a triangular or square wave,

Square LFO wave causes the pitch to switch rapidly between two notes, called a trill.

Lower pitch   Higher pitch

High volume

Low volume

Here, an LFO wave is mixed with the wave from the amplifier. The note rapidly varies in volume, called tremolo.

PULSE CODE MODULATION

You can vary the width of a square wave so it becomes rectangular, called pulse width modulation. This alters the sound.

Square wave produces clarinet-type sound.

Rectangular wave sounds like an oboe.

RING MODULATION

This has a haunting quality, like bells.

This modulation produces a metallic, beating sound, like a distorted electric guitar.

SYNCHRONIZATION

DETUNING

Two oscillators produce waves at different pitches. Combining them gives a fatter sound as the number of harmonics is increased.

TRANSPOSING

This raises or lowers the pitch of all the notes.

The digital signal is now made into a different type of signal, called an analogue signal. This is sent to the speaker, which turns it into a sound wave that you can hear.

17

Keyboard synthesizers

On these two pages you can find out about the kind of keyboards that are called keyboard synthesizers, or just synthesizers. These are the kind of instruments you see pop groups and bands using. They cost about three or four times as much as the average portable keyboard.

Synthesizers have their own built-in "sound factories" similar to those on the previous pages. They can do a lot more, though, and have many extra controls.

There are three main types of synthesizer: preset, variable and programmable.

Preset synthesizers

These are like portable keyboards, only they can produce a much better sound quality. They have up to 128 preset (stored) sounds which cannot be changed.

Variable synthesizers

Each sound control, or parameter, on these keyboards can be changed using the dials and knobs on the synthesizer. Sounds cannot be stored and you cannot change easily from one to another.

Programmable synthesizers

These are the most common type of synthesizer. They can have as many as 128 preset sounds. New sounds can be made either by changing these, or starting from scratch. They can then be stored and called up when needed. All this is done using the programming unit.

You can usually play up to eight notes at once on programmable synthesizers (i.e. they are polyphonic). In the picture you can see a programmable synthesizer. The labels explain some of the things it can do.

Each parameter, or control, has a number. To alter the value of a parameter, you type in its number on the programming unit.

The value of the parameter is altered using the ADJUST buttons.

Programming unit is used to select presets and make new sounds.

You type in the number of the preset sound you want using these buttons.

Window displays preset number.

Parameter windows display the number of the parameter being changed and its value.

Some synthesizers show the parameter values by fluorescent displays.

Tuning wheel can be adjusted so that the synthesizer can play in tune with other instruments.

This dial makes the notes slide from one to another. This is called portamento. The dial also varies the speed of the slide.

Performance controls (joystick and dials) affect the sound while it is being made.

The bottom left button in the programming unit is called the WRITE button. It stores the values of parameters to form a new preset.

Joystick makes the pitch rise or fall if moved side to side. If moved up it gives a tremolo (wavering volume) effect and if moved down, vibrato (wavering pitch). Some synthesizers use two wheels instead of a joystick (see next page).

Some keyboards can be played like this. The performance controls are on a detachable handgrip.

Envelope generator

Some synthesizers have special envelope generators, for both the timbre and the volume, which enable them to imitate instruments even better. They have two more stages than the ADSR type (see page 16).

Decay

Slope. This stage controls how quickly the volume changes between the break point and sustain levels.

Sustain

Break point. When the volume has fallen to a certain level in the decay stage, called the break point, it enters another stage, called the slope stage.

Attack

Release

Decay

Attack

Slope gives second decay like on a real piano.

This kind of envelope is known as ADBSSR. In the picture you can see how it can be used to produce a piano envelope.

Some synthesizers have a slot for cartridges containing more presets. The player can also store music on them.

Sockets to link to other equipment. This is explained on page 24.

A foot pedal can be plugged in here. It enables the player to change the preset without having to stop playing. It can also be used to make the notes sound for longer, called sustain.

Headphones can be plugged in here to enable the player to practise without being heard.

Sockets for tape machine on which can be stored presets or music.

If you keep your fingers on the keys after the note has sounded, and then press harder, you get a vibrato (varying volume) effect while the note is sounding. This is called after-touch.

Envelope generators, explained above.

Many synthesizers have a sequencer which can store a number of musical parts. The music can be played back by pressing a button. Another part can be played on top of it "live".

Split keyboard. The synthesizer allows the player to use a different preset with different sections of the keyboard (how many depends on the synthesizer). The split points are usually set by the player.

Touch sensitivity. The keys are sensitive to how they are pressed. Pressing hard produces a louder sound, called pressure sensitivity. Pressing quickly can produce a sharp sound. This is velocity sensitivity. These enable more "feeling" to be put into the music.

You may see a keyboard player with two synthesizers arranged like this. The top one is monophonic and is extremely good at synthesis, so it is used to play melody lines.

19

Digital synthesizers

Digital synthesizers are a type of programmable synthesizer. They use additive synthesis, where sound waves are added together to make new sounds. This gives the player a great deal of control over the sounds being made. They can produce excellent imitations of musical instruments.

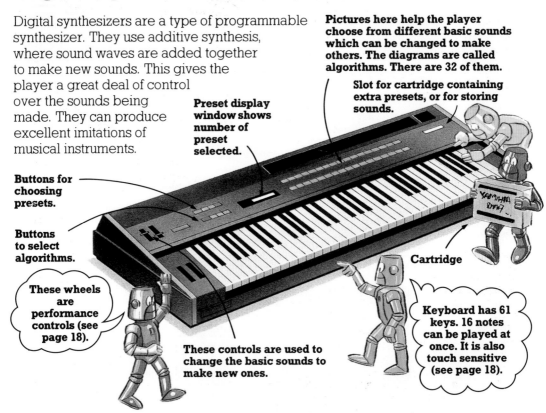

Pictures here help the player choose from different basic sounds which can be changed to make others. The diagrams are called algorithms. There are 32 of them.

Slot for cartridge containing extra presets, or for storing sounds.

Preset display window shows number of preset selected.

Buttons for choosing presets.

Buttons to select algorithms.

These wheels are performance controls (see page 18).

These controls are used to change the basic sounds to make new ones.

Cartridge

Keyboard has 61 keys. 16 notes can be played at once. It is also touch sensitive (see page 18).

In the picture above you can see a Yamaha DX7. This uses a new type of additive synthesis called Frequency Modulated (FM) digital synthesis. This enables the volume and timbre of a note to be changed all the time it is sounding, making it sound just like a musical instrument playing a note.

Music computers

Some home computers are specially designed for digital music synthesis. They have very powerful synthesizer chips.

Single finger chords and bass.

Cartridge

50 presets

8 notes can be played at once.

Split keyboard at any point.

Stores up to 2,000 notes.

6 preset rhythms

The Yamaha CX5M is an MSX machine costing about twice as much as the average home computer. It has a similar synthesizer chip to the Yamaha DX9. You can buy a keyboard which plugs into the side so you can use it as a synthesizer.

You can buy software cartridges for the CX5M. One cartridge enables you to store (or sequence) up to eight musical parts in step time. The music appears on the screen as you write it. Another allows you to create your own sounds. Yet another lets you connect it to a Yamaha DX7 and use all its functions.

Non-keyboard synthesizers

Not all synthesizers are in the form of keyboards. There are drum synthesizers, guitar synthesizers and others, too. You can find out about these on the next three pages.

Guitar synthesizers

A guitar synthesizer works like a keyboard synthesizer, except that notes are played by plucking guitar strings. Signals from the strings are then sent to the floor synthesizer unit where the sounds are made.

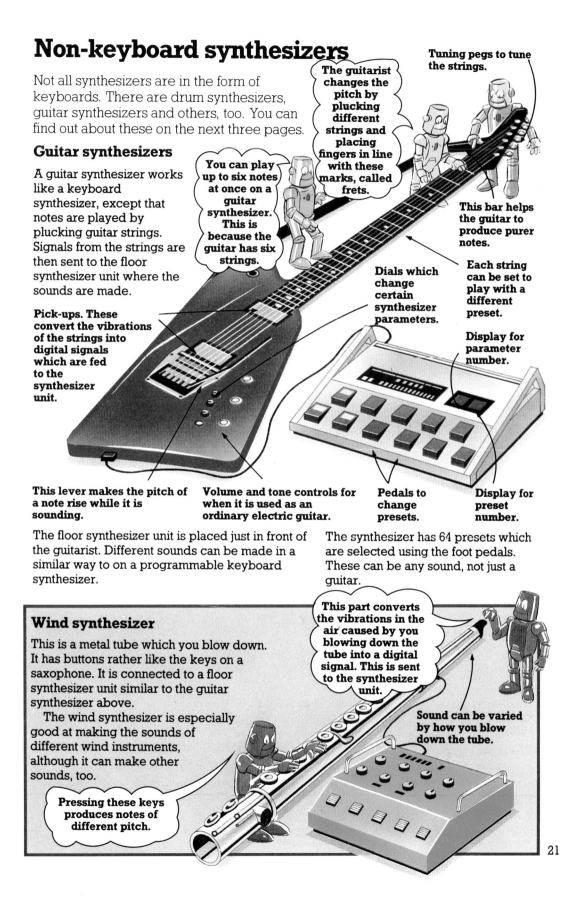

Tuning pegs to tune the strings.

The guitarist changes the pitch by plucking different strings and placing fingers in line with these marks, called frets.

You can play up to six notes at once on a guitar synthesizer. This is because the guitar has six strings.

This bar helps the guitar to produce purer notes.

Dials which change certain synthesizer parameters.

Each string can be set to play with a different preset.

Display for parameter number.

Pick-ups. These convert the vibrations of the strings into digital signals which are fed to the synthesizer unit.

This lever makes the pitch of a note rise while it is sounding.

Volume and tone controls for when it is used as an ordinary electric guitar.

Pedals to change presets.

Display for preset number.

The floor synthesizer unit is placed just in front of the guitarist. Different sounds can be made in a similar way to on a programmable keyboard synthesizer.

The synthesizer has 64 presets which are selected using the foot pedals. These can be any sound, not just a guitar.

Wind synthesizer

This is a metal tube which you blow down. It has buttons rather like the keys on a saxophone. It is connected to a floor synthesizer unit similar to the guitar synthesizer above.

The wind synthesizer is especially good at making the sounds of different wind instruments, although it can make other sounds, too.

This part converts the vibrations in the air caused by you blowing down the tube into a digital signal. This is sent to the synthesizer unit.

Sound can be varied by how you blow down the tube.

Pressing these keys produces notes of different pitch.

21

Electronic drums

Electronic drums are played in the same way as ordinary drums. They can produce all sorts of different sounds, though, as they are connected to a drum synthesizer. You can tell if a drummer is playing electronic drums as they are much flatter than ordinary ones. They are also usually six-sided instead of round and the tops of the drums, called pads, are black.

When the drum is struck, signals are sent to a synthesizer unit. In the picture you can see an electronic drum kit and synthesizer.

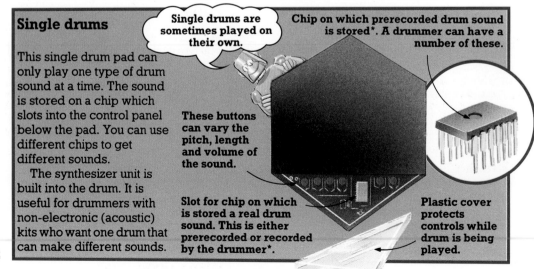

Pads are hit with ordinary drum sticks.

This slot is for a special chip which contains the prerecorded sound of a real drum*. The sound is played when one of the drums is hit.

Headphones let a drummer practise without anyone else being able to hear.

Electronic cymbals. These are pads used to make cymbal sounds.

Drum pads are made from very tough rubber. They are touch sensitive.

The synthesizer unit is usually on the floor next to the drummer.

Bass drum. Drummer uses a foot pedal to hit this.

The drum synthesizer unit contains a number of preset drum sounds. The drummer can either use these or program different ones.

Foot switch to change the presets on the drum pads.

Each drum can make a different kind of drum sound. The synthesizer can store up to 20 sets of sounds. Each set contains the sounds for all the drums. Drummers can use different "drum kits" for different musical styles (e.g. reggae, rock and so on). A foot switch enables the drummer to change from one kit to another.

Single drums

Single drums are sometimes played on their own.

Chip on which prerecorded drum sound is stored*. A drummer can have a number of these.

This single drum pad can only play one type of drum sound at a time. The sound is stored on a chip which slots into the control panel below the pad. You can use different chips to get different sounds.

The synthesizer unit is built into the drum. It is useful for drummers with non-electronic (acoustic) kits who want one drum that can make different sounds.

These buttons can vary the pitch, length and volume of the sound.

Slot for chip on which is stored a real drum sound. This is either prerecorded or recorded by the drummer*.

Plastic cover protects controls while drum is being played.

*There is more about recording real sounds to use with synthesizers on pages 26-27.

Rhythm machines

Many pop groups and bands use rhythm machines to play the drum part for their songs. Rhythm machines can imitate the sounds of different percussion instruments (i.e. those that make sound when something is struck such as drums, tambourines or maracas). The most expensive machines use prerecorded* sounds. These cost as much as a keyboard synthesizer.

The sounds they produce are so realistic that it is often hard to tell if the drum beat in a song is a rhythm machine or a real drummer.

A rhythm machine can store the percussion parts to 99 different songs.

Controls to alter the volume of each sound.

This dial sets the tempo, or speed, of the rhythm.

Window displays rhythms in sections called bars. You can use preset (stored) rhythms or record your own in step or real time. This is explained below.

Slot for cartridge to record rhythm patterns on.

Some machines have a tuning dial to vary the pitch of a sound.

Button for each different percussion sound. These include sounds like "hand clap".

Setting rhythms in step time

Each section of rhythm, or bar, is divided into 16 steps. The drummer tells the machine which instrument should sound on each step.

This dot shows that the bass drum will sound on step one.

Each of the 16 steps is indicated in turn by a light.

The instrument buttons are pressed to set a sound for the step indicated.

Pad programmers

There is another kind of rhythm machine called a pad programmer. You can store rhythms by tapping on its pads with your fingers or drum sticks.

The stored rhythm for one bar is called a pattern. Preset and programmed patterns can be repeated to make up the drum part for a whole song.

Patterns

Setting rhythms in real time

The drummer taps out the rhythm on the buttons. The machine helps him to keep in time by providing a regular beat called a click track, the speed of which can be varied. The machine corrects the rhythm to the nearest sixteenth part of a bar if it is not quite on the beat.

SONG

Rhythm machines and synthesizers can be used to control other electronic instruments. You can find out about this on the next page.

23

Connecting electronic instruments

A musician can connect together various electronic instruments, e.g. synthesizer and rhythm machine, and control them all from one place. This is done by using MIDI (Musical Instrument Digital Interface).

An interface is a piece of electronic circuitry which enables one piece of equipment to be connected to, and work with, another. It takes the signal from one and changes it into a form that can be understood by the other. This is like saying that MIDI allows electronic instruments to speak the same language.

MIDI can either be built into an instrument, or bought as a separate unit*. MIDI can also link home computers to electronic instruments, enabling them to control powerful synthesizers.

How MIDI works

There are two types of information that MIDI sends from one piece of equipment to another. They are shown on the right.

1. System codes
These codes are all the music instructions for the instrument. They include pitches of notes, speed, parameter levels, touch sensitivity, and so on.

2. Channel code
This is a code which ensures the information goes to the right instrument. Each instrument has its own channel code.

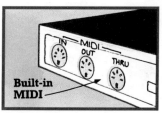

Information is transferred from one piece of equipment to another by means of three sockets. These are labelled "IN", "OUT" and "THRU".

The IN and OUT sockets are like the earpiece and mouthpiece on a telephone. The IN receives the information, and the OUT sends it.

If the information is not for a particular instrument, the THRU socket allows the information to pass through without affecting it.

Connecting synthesizers

The synthesizers in this picture have built-in MIDI. They are connected so that by playing on either one, the musician can also control the other. One synthesizer might be playing a string sound and the other a brass sound. If each has eight note polyphony, then sixteen notes can be played at once.

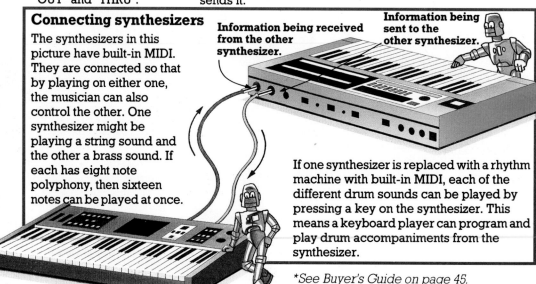

Information being received from the other synthesizer.

Information being sent to the other synthesizer.

If one synthesizer is replaced with a rhythm machine with built-in MIDI, each of the different drum sounds can be played by pressing a key on the synthesizer. This means a keyboard player can program and play drum accompaniments from the synthesizer.

*See Buyer's Guide on page 45.

More MIDI connections

If you see a musician on the television or in concert using a number of different electronic instruments, they will all be connected with MIDI. Up to 16 electronic instruments, in many combinations can be connected with MIDI. This picture shows MIDI linking a computer to various instruments.

Part of the system codes are signals to start the instruments in the arrangement, called triggers. These are sent from the computer or synthesizer.

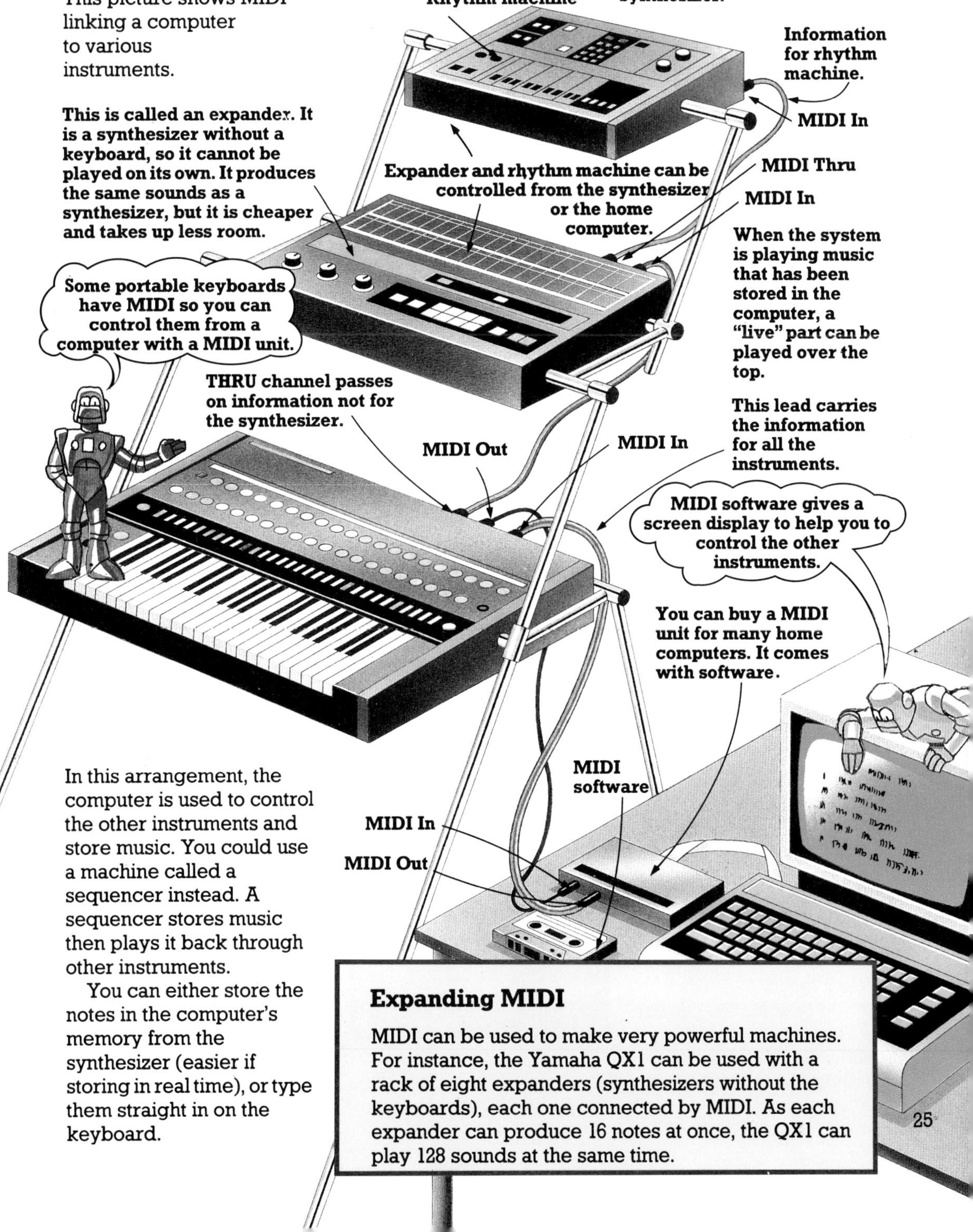

Rhythm machine

Information for rhythm machine.

MIDI In

This is called an expander. It is a synthesizer without a keyboard, so it cannot be played on its own. It produces the same sounds as a synthesizer, but it is cheaper and takes up less room.

Expander and rhythm machine can be controlled from the synthesizer or the home computer.

MIDI Thru

MIDI In

When the system is playing music that has been stored in the computer, a "live" part can be played over the top.

Some portable keyboards have MIDI so you can control them from a computer with a MIDI unit.

THRU channel passes on information not for the synthesizer.

MIDI Out

MIDI In

This lead carries the information for all the instruments.

MIDI software gives a screen display to help you to control the other instruments.

You can buy a MIDI unit for many home computers. It comes with software.

MIDI software

In this arrangement, the computer is used to control the other instruments and store music. You could use a machine called a sequencer instead. A sequencer stores music then plays it back through other instruments.

MIDI In

MIDI Out

You can either store the notes in the computer's memory from the synthesizer (easier if storing in real time), or type them straight in on the keyboard.

Expanding MIDI

MIDI can be used to make very powerful machines. For instance, the Yamaha QX1 can be used with a rack of eight expanders (synthesizers without the keyboards), each one connected by MIDI. As each expander can produce 16 notes at once, the QX1 can play 128 sounds at the same time.

25

Sampling

Real, live sounds can be stored in a computer's or synthesizer's memory using a method called sampling. Instead of the computer creating sound waves to imitate real sounds as in synthesis, sampling lets you use actual sounds.

All sounds are made up of waves, whether they come from a musical instrument, a door slamming or you talking. Once the sound is stored inside the computer, the wave can be altered in a number of ways. For instance, you can change the pitch of the sound so that you can play tunes with it.

On the next two pages you can find out about sampling on home computers, special sampling keyboards and large, very expensive machines called computer musical instruments.

Sampling on a home computer

Sampled sounds are replayed through loudspeaker.

Microphone   Sampling hardware

You can buy a sampling system for most home computers. It usually consists of a piece of hardware and some software.

The computer "hears" the sound through a microphone. Sampling takes up a lot of memory space, so you can usually only record up to four seconds of sound. This is long enough for most sounds that you would want to sample, though.

Using sampled sounds

Below, you can see some of the things you can do with a sampled sound once it is in the computer's memory.

Different pitches

You can play tunes using the sound you have sampled. The software enables you to type in the notes in the same way as step time sequencing (see page 9).

Reverse

You can get some interesting sounds by reversing samples, that is, playing them back to front.

Part sound

You can store up to four short sounds. The software lets you play them back on different keys. You might use this to make a drum kit, each key being a different drum.

Lengthening and shortening

The sound can be replayed over a longer or shorter period of time. You can use this to turn a sample of a match being struck into a sizzling thunderbolt. If it is replayed in a shorter time, it sounds like a gun shot.

Looping

You can choose any part of the sound to replay in a loop, so it is constantly repeated.

Riser

This replays the sound in a loop with rising pitch.

Echo

The computer can make the sounds echo. The software lets you vary the amount of echo.

Chorai

This makes a single sound into a multiple one.

Sampling keyboards

Sampling keyboards can use sampled sounds to play music. In the picture below is a Fairlight CMI (Computer Musical Instrument). It costs more than a hundred home computers. As well as sampling, it allows players to create amazing sounds by drawing waves on the screen with a special pen, called a light pen.

Many pop groups use Fairlights to write, play and record their songs. It is such a powerful machine that it can be used to create and store the soundtrack for a whole film. Other sampling keyboard systems you may find on record sleeves are the Emulator II and the Synclavier.

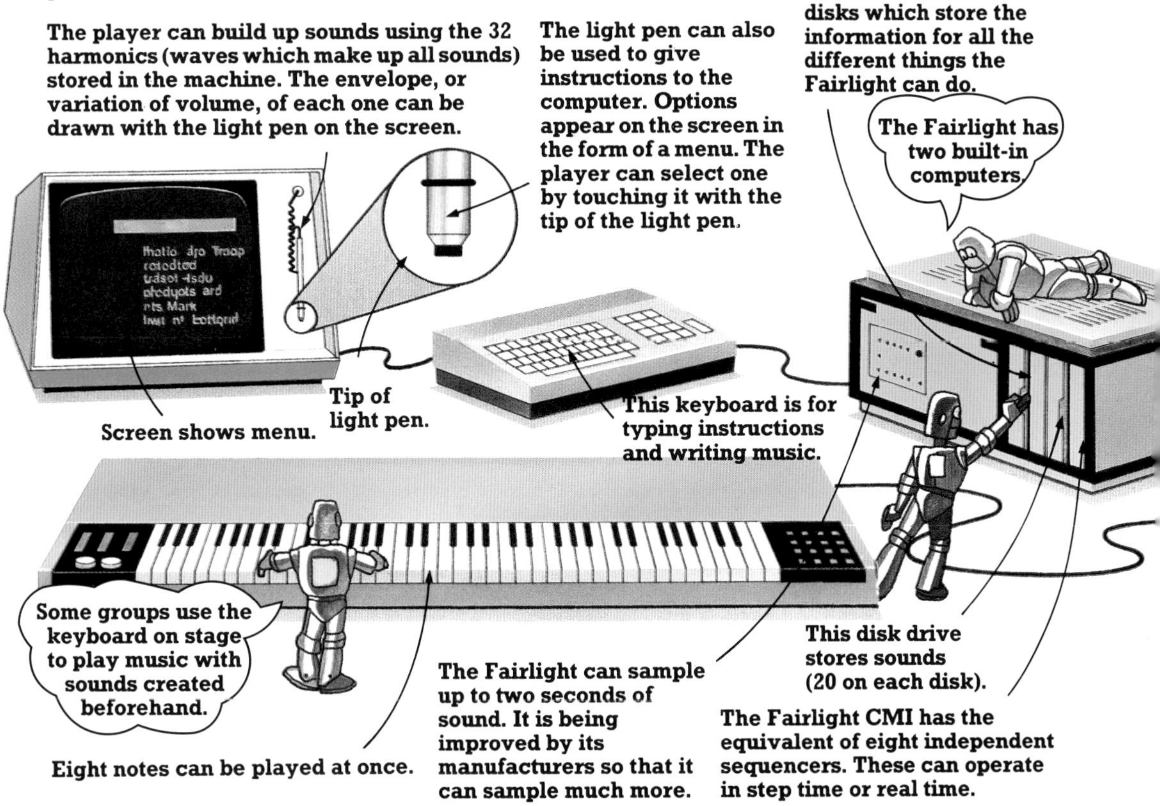

The player can build up sounds using the 32 harmonics (waves which make up all sounds) stored in the machine. The envelope, or variation of volume, of each one can be drawn with the light pen on the screen.

The light pen can also be used to give instructions to the computer. Options appear on the screen in the form of a menu. The player can select one by touching it with the tip of the light pen.

This disk drive is for disks which store the information for all the different things the Fairlight can do.

The Fairlight has two built-in computers.

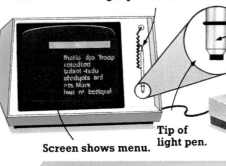

Screen shows menu.

Tip of light pen.

This keyboard is for typing instructions and writing music.

Some groups use the keyboard on stage to play music with sounds created beforehand.

Eight notes can be played at once.

The Fairlight can sample up to two seconds of sound. It is being improved by its manufacturers so that it can sample much more.

This disk drive stores sounds (20 on each disk).

The Fairlight CMI has the equivalent of eight independent sequencers. These can operate in step time or real time.

Drawing waves and creating sounds

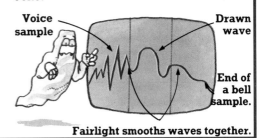

The player can draw a sound wave on the screen using the light pen, then replay it to hear the sound. Part or all of the sound can be redrawn to improve it. This sound can then be mixed and merged with sampled or created waves to make unique, complex sounds and effects.

In the picture below, the drawn wave of an electronic whistling sound can be added to that of someone talking. The Fairlight will smoothly join the waves together, and the result might be a ghostly voice. If the wave of the ring of a bell dying away is added at the end, the sound will have a haunting echo.

Voice sample

Drawn wave

End of a bell sample.

Fairlight smooths waves together.

How to compose your own music

There are many different ways to compose music without necessarily being able to play a musical instrument.

On the next six pages are some guidelines as to how to go about composing your own music, starting with the tune, then building up the rhythm, bass part and harmony. To help you, there is information on music keyboards and writing music down.

If you have a portable keyboard, computer or a piano, you can use it to play the music in this section.

Finally, you can find out how to add words, or lyrics, to make the music into a song.

Making up tunes in real time

The simplest way to compose music is to make up a tune in your head and tape yourself humming it.

When you are pleased with what you have made up, you can either record it (on tape, computer or keyboard), or write it down.*

If you have a tune in your head, or on tape, you can try to pick it out on your keyboard.

Alternatively, you can start to write the tune by playing different notes on your keyboard.

Try playing a few notes at a time until you play something that you like. You can then build on this.

Making up tunes in step time

You can only make up tunes in step time if you have a computer and sequencing software, like that on page 38. If portable keyboards let you store tunes, it is usually in real time (i.e. by playing it live).

You can either store a tune that you have previously composed and written down*, or you can try different things to hear what they sound like.

The notes have to be entered one at a time on either a music or computer keyboard. With most software you have to write down a pitch, length and octave (see page 9).

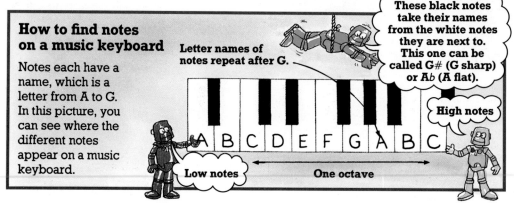

How to find notes on a music keyboard

Notes each have a name, which is a letter from A to G. In this picture, you can see where the different notes appear on a music keyboard.

Letter names of notes repeat after G.

These black notes take their names from the white notes they are next to. This one can be called G# (G sharp) or Ab (A flat).

High notes

A B C D E F G A B C

Low notes

One octave

*You can find out how to write music down on the next page.

Musical parts

Most music is made up of more than one part. For instance, a pop group may have a guitar, synthesizer, drums and bass guitar all playing different parts. When they are all played together, they make one piece of music.

To compose music, you can start with any part, then build up the others. Most composers begin with the tune.

There is no "right" or "wrong" music. A lot depends on your taste. Don't be afraid to keep the tune simple. The best music is often based on the simplest patterns of notes.

This is the part that you will probably sing to represent the whole of a piece of music. It is also called the melody. It is quite important that the tune is "catchy".

Writing down your tune

If you want to write down your tune, you can write the names of the notes (see previous page). For instance, the note names for the first two lines of the French folk song "Frère Jacques" are:

All the notes have the same length.

CDEC, CDEC

Writing these notes is quite easy as each one is in the same octave and has the same length. Tunes made up of notes of different lengths, in different octaves and with lots of sharps and flats, are more complicated.

There is a special way of writing music down, which tells you what notes to play and how to play them. Music is written on lines called staves. You can see these in the picture below.

Notes can be added to the top and bottom of the staves by drawing in lines, like the one on which middle C is drawn. These are called ledger lines.

Stave. Each line and space represents a different key on the music keyboard.

Notice that the lines and spaces on the two clefs represent different note names.

These are the note names which each line and space represents.

This note is called middle C. It is the nearest C to the centre of most music keyboards.

Treble clef. This indicates that the notes on this stave are on the upper part of the keyboard. Notes written on this stave are usually played with the right hand.

Sharps and flats (usually black notes) are indicated on the stave by their sign being put before the note. This is C#.

Bass clef. This indicates that the notes on the stave are on the lower part of the keyboard. Notes written on this stave are usually played with the left hand.

When you are writing a tune, you usually only use the top stave. The bottom one is for bass notes.

Writing music on staves

On this page you can find out how to write music on staves. On the stave below is the music for the first two lines of "Frère Jacques". The note names of this tune are written on the previous page.

This is called the time signature. The top number tells you how many beats are in a bar, or section. The bottom number tells you what length beat they are. There is more about time signatures on the next page.

The shape of the note tells you its length. This note has a length of one beat, and is called a crotchet (quarter note*). There is a table of some of the note lengths below.

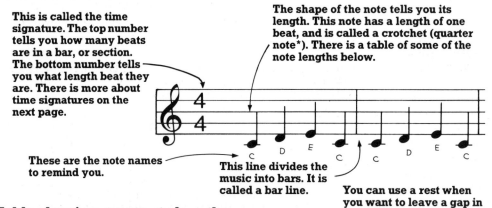

These are the note names to remind you.

This line divides the music into bars. It is called a bar line.

You can use a rest when you want to leave a gap in the music.

Table showing some note lengths

Symbol	Name	Length (Number of beats)	Rest symbol	Symbol	Name	Length (Number of beats)	Rest symbol
𝆺	Semibreve (Whole note)	Four	▭	♩	Crotchet (Quarter note)	One	𝄽
♩	Minim (Half note)	Two	▭	♪	Quaver (Eighth note)	Half	𝄾

Below is the tune of a song that has been specially composed for this book. If you have a computer, you can store the tune a note at a time by using the program on page 38.

You can also practise playing it "live". There are numbers under the music which will help you count the beats. The beats are regular, like a clock ticking.

You may need to count these numbers out loud to start with, to help you play the right note lengths. Later, you can count silently in your head.

This dot means that the note is made longer by half. This dotted minim (half note*) is three beats long.

This rest is one beat long.

The "tails" of the notes point down when the notes are above the middle line of the stave.

On the next four pages are other red boxes which show you how to add the rhythm, bass, harmony and words to this tune.

Dotted crotchet (quarter note) is one and a half beats long.

This quaver (eighth note*) is half a beat long. Count an "and" between beats 2 and 3 to keep it in time.

Double bar line is put at the end of the music.

*In the US and Canada, the notes are known by the names in brackets.

Rhythm provides a regular beat for music. It is the part you will probably tap your foot or fingers in time to. Rhythm is usually played on percussion instruments, i.e. those where sound is made by something being either struck (e.g. a drum) or strummed (e.g. a guitar).

Tapping and writing rhythms

You can tap out a rhythm on anything using your fingers. Rhythms can be written down in the same way as other music except that rhythm symbols are used.

On the right are some rhythms for you to try. To help you, notes of different lengths are written in different colours, and they also have the word "tap" written underneath them.

Usually the first beat of the bar is stronger than the others. This may be indicated by this sign, called an accent.

The time signature for this rhythm is 3/4.

One beat TAP

These words tell you when to tap.

It is very important that the rhythm part keeps a regular beat.

When two quavers (half beat notes) are used together, their tails are joined.

One beat rests

When you are writing rhythms to tap out, you do not have to use a clef as the notes have no pitch.

You can repeat these bars several times over.

This is one of the rhythms in the program on page 38.

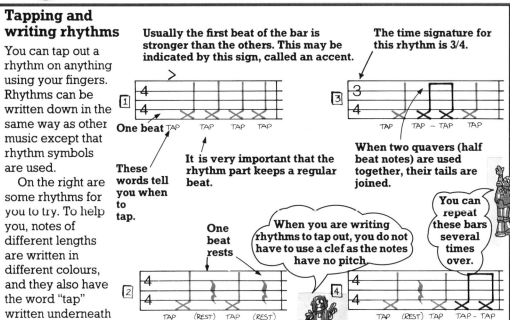

Rhythms for more than one instrument

You can use the third space up on the stave to write a rhythm for a second rhythm instrument. Try the rhythms below with two "drums". The music tells you with which hand to tap each note.

Try tapping a table top with your right hand and a tray with your left.

Right hand tap

Left hand tap

This note is not on the regular beat. It is called an off-beat. Rhythms which have off-beats are called syncopated rhythms.

This is a half beat rest.

A rhythm for the tune

There are many rhythms which can be used for the tune on the previous page. Here is one of them.

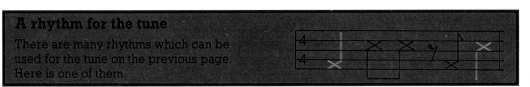

THE BASS

The bass part is the lowest in pitch. It is the part played by a bass guitar or the left hand on a piano. In order to play the melody and bass parts together, you need a keyboard which lets you play at least two notes at once.

Single-note bass

Some bass parts consist of only one note at a time. On the right is a simple bass part for the tune. The bass notes are written on the bottom stave. There is one note for every bar.

If you find it hard to play with two hands, try recording the melody and working out bass notes when you play it back.

Usually the bass note will sound right with a bar containing mostly notes from its chord (see below).

Many tunes have more than one note per bar in the bass part.

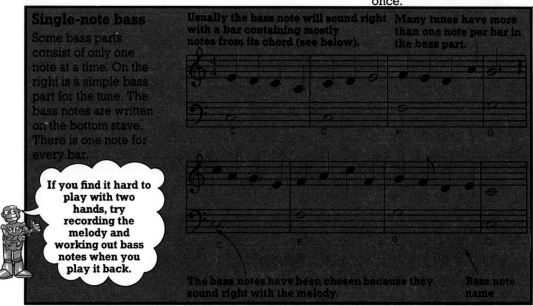

The bass notes have been chosen because they sound right with the melody.

Bass note name

Working out chords

You can play more than one note at a time in the bass part. Multiple notes are called chords. In the picture on the right you can see how to work out the simplest three-note chord. This is the chord of C major.

The distance between two adjacent notes is called a semitone.

All major chords can be worked out this way.

The note at the bottom is C.

The middle note is worked out by counting up four notes (including black ones) from the bass note.

The top note is three notes above that.

The chord of C major is written like this.

You can just write the letter name of the chord.

Scales

A scale is eight notes covering one octave, with a set pattern of semitones and tones (two semitones) between them.

In the picture on the right you can see the simplest scale which is C major. It consists of all the white notes between two C notes.

Tone   Semitone

The first, third and fifth notes of a major scale make a major chord.

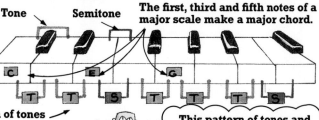

Pattern of tones and semitones.

All music is based on the set of notes in a scale. The tune above is based on those in C major.

This pattern of tones and semitones is the same for major scales starting on any note. This means that some will include black notes.
Try working out the scale of G major. Which black notes does it contain? Answer on the next page.

32

THE HARMONY

The harmony is the part which fits in with the melody and makes it sound more interesting; for instance, it can make your tune sound happy or sad.

Trying different harmonies

Harmony occurs when at least two notes are played at the same time. The harmony part often uses the same sequence of note lengths as the melody, but the pitches are different.

Two notes played at the same time can sound pleasant or harsh, depending on the number of notes, called the interval, between them. When you are working out a harmony, you can choose notes which suit the style of the music you are writing. The picture on the right shows you which intervals sound good and which do not.

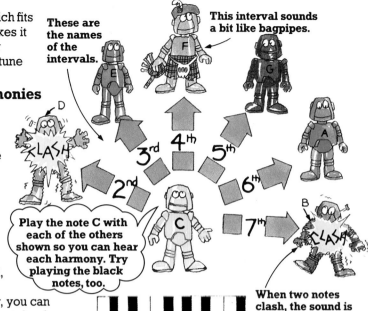

These are the names of the intervals.

This interval sounds a bit like bagpipes.

Play the note C with each of the others shown so you can hear each harmony. Try playing the black notes, too.

When two notes clash, the sound is called a discord.

Writing a harmony

As with all music composition, the best way to learn to write harmonies is to experiment. The simplest kind of harmony, which works with many tunes, is to play the melody line a third higher. On the right is one possible harmony to the tune on the previous page.

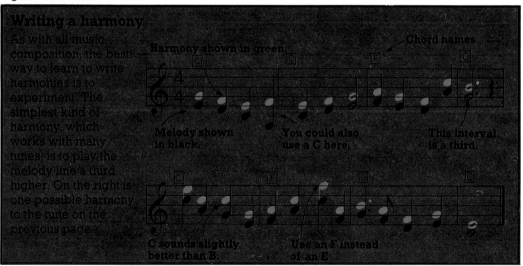

Harmony shown in green.

Chord names.

Melody shown in black.

You could also use a C here.

This interval is a third.

C sounds slightly better than B.

Use an F instead of an E.

Answer to the question on page 32

There is an F sharp in G major.

If you want to write a tune based on the notes in the scale of G major, you put a # sign on the F line of the stave at the beginning of the music. This is called the key signature. The music is said to be "in the key of G major".

This tells you to play F# instead of F throughout the whole tune.

Sharp sign on the line representing F.

Each scale has a different number of sharps or flats. You can tell from the key signature what scale the music is based on.

Writing your own songs

You can add words, called lyrics, to your tune to make a song. There are no rules for writing songs. Sometimes you might get an idea for the lyrics first, and other times the music.

VERSES
The main sections.

CHORUS
This is repeated between verses.

INSTRUMENTAL
This is just music without any words. It is used between verses and at the beginning and end of a song.

Song patterns

Songs can include any or all of the sections shown on the right.

Adding lyrics to music

Below you can see three examples of how lyrics can be added to the tune on the opposite page.

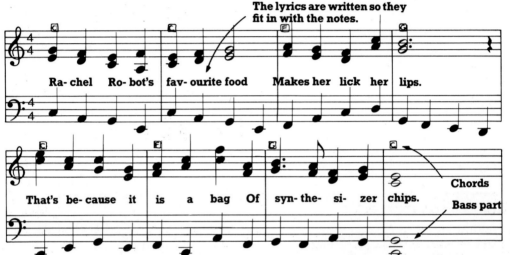

The lyrics are written so they fit in with the notes.

Ra- chel Ro- bot's fav- ourite food Makes her lick her lips.

That's be- cause it is a bag Of syn- the- si- zer chips.

Chords

Bass part

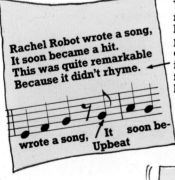

Rachel Robot wrote a song,
It soon became a hit.
This was quite remarkable
Because it didn't rhyme.

wrote a song, It soon be-
Upbeat

You can put in extra notes to match the lyrics. This particular note is called an upbeat as it is just before the first beat of a new bar.

Songs sound better if they rhyme. You can buy a rhyming dictionary to help you.

Stephen Stickley got a tan,
One bright and sunny day.
Big black rain clouds came along
And washed it all away.

Each of these three songs could be a verse, chorus or a whole song. Try writing your own lyrics to the tune. You could write them about your family or friends.

Types of songs

You can write songs to express a mood. In the picture below you can see some different types of songs with features that they might have.

HAPPY
Quick tempo and catchy melody.

SAD
Slow tempo and smooth, flowing music.

ROMANTIC
Quite slow with gentle rhythm.

HUMOUROUS
Quite quick tempo and a simple melody as the lyrics are important.

ANGRY
Jerky rhythm, discords, loud.

A music program for you to run

In this section of the book there is a music program which you can run on your computer. It is both a synthesis and a sequencing program.

The program will run on the Commodore 64, Spectrum, BBC, VIC 20, Electron and MSX. It is listed on page 38. Conversions for the different computers are listed after the main program.

With it, you can play your computer like a musical instrument using five preset sounds. You can record tunes by either playing notes, or typing in their names. You can also add a rhythm to your tune, and edit it.

The synthesizer chips in the Spectrum and the VIC 20 mean there can be no presets. There are no rhythms on the Electron or MSX. The Spectrum cannot provide rhythms or presets.

How to use the program

Type in the program (taking care to include all the relevant conversions for your computer). When you run it, you will see:

```
SELECT TIME:
1 = 4/4
2 = 3/4
?
```

Type 1 or 2 to select time signature and press **RETURN**.

You must always press RETURN after typing in an answer to a question, i.e. when you see ?.

You will see an arrow in the top left-hand corner of the screen. This means you are in **Music Command Mode**. There are a number of music commands, which are explained below. You can use any of them when you see an arrow. There is a table of them on page 40.

Playing music

Here are the commands you need to play music on your computer.

You do not need to press RETURN after typing in a music command.

```
->S    PRESET SOUND

SELECT PRESET (1-5)
?
```
You can choose from five presets. Type in the number of the one you want (and press RETURN).

```
->T    TEMPO

SET TEMPO: (1 - 15)
?
```
1 is very slow and 15 is very fast. If you do not set a tempo, the computer will automatically set it to 5.

Tempo is a musical term meaning speed.

```
->K    KEYBOARD

KEYBOARD:
RECORD?
1 = ON
0 = OFF
?
```
Press 0 (and RETURN) to play on the keyboard without recording. You can find out what happens if you press 1 on the next page.

Below is a picture showing which keys play which musical notes. The computer will display each note as you play it.

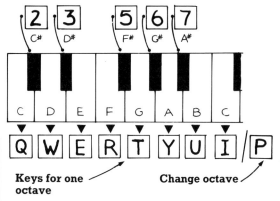

Keys for one octave — Change octave

The program has a range of two octaves but the keyboard only has the keys for one. When you start, the keyboard will play the lower octave, octave 1. You press P to switch between them. When you have finished playing, press RETURN to get back to music command mode.

Recording tunes by playing notes

To begin with you press **K**, then type in 1 (and press RETURN) to record what you play on the keyboard. You will be asked:

```
START FROM?
```

You now type in the number of the note from which you wish to begin. If you are starting at the beginning, type 1 (and press RETURN).

```
B-1 C-1 D-2 C-1 F#1 RST F-2 C-3
```

You can now play notes as before, only this time the computer will remember them. If you press the space bar, you record a rest (i.e. a note with a length, or duration, but no pitch). Press RETURN when you have finished.

You can leave as long as you like between playing notes as the computer gives them all a duration of 1 beat.

Below are some other commands which you can use.

->L   LIST

```
TIME 4/4
-------------- 1
 1    C-1   1
 2    D-1   1
 3    E-1   2
-------------- 2
 4    F-1   2
```

Lists all the notes you have played in numbered order. Lists up to 11 notes on one page in whole bars, which are also numbered. Press any key to list bars on the next page.

—> If you press RETURN on any page, you get back to music command mode and the page remains displayed. This is useful for editing.

->R   RHYTHM

```
0 = OFF
1 = RHYTHM 1
2 = RHYTHM 2
?
```

This turns the rhythm on or off. If you have chosen 4/4 time, you can also choose between two different rhythms.

->P   PLAY

Plays whatever is stored in the computer's memory and the rhythm, if you have turned it on. Press RETURN to stop play.

You can find out how to edit your tune on the next page.

Recording tunes by typing in note names

You have to type in the pitch and duration of each note. To do this, you press **N** (see below). Before you do, though, you may like to see a menu of the notes by pressing **M**.

->M   MENU

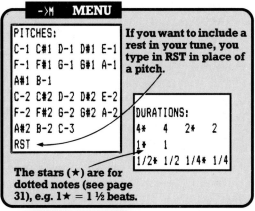

```
PITCHES:
C-1 C#1 D-1 D#1 E-1
F-1 F#1 G-1 G#1 A-1
A#1 B-1
C-2 C#2 D-2 D#2 E-2
F-2 F#2 G-2 G#2 A-2
A#2 B-2 C-3
RST
```

```
DURATIONS:
4*   4   2*   2
1*   1
1/2* 1/2 1/4* 1/4
```

If you want to include a rest in your tune, you type in RST in place of a pitch.

The stars (*) are for dotted notes (see page 31), e.g. 1* = 1 ½ beats.

->C   CLEAR

If you have already recorded a tune, you can clear the computer's memory by typing **C**.

```
ARE YOU SURE (Y/N)?
Y
```

Type Y to clear the memory and reset the rhythm, time, preset and tempo.

->N   NEW NOTE

```
START FROM?1
1:?
```

If you are beginning your tune, type 1. (If not, type in the number of the note from which you wish to resume.)

The computer is waiting for you to type in your first note.

Pitch

```
1:?C-2.1
2:?D#2.1
```

Press RETURN after each note and when you have finished.

Duration

Full stop

Note that with sharps (#), there is no hyphen (-).

The notes should be typed in the form in which they appear in the menu.

ERRORS

```
1:?C-2.1000
DURATION ERROR
1:?
```

If you make a mistake, the computer will print PITCH ERROR or DURATION ERROR. You then re-type the note.

Bars

The computer puts in bar lines every three or four beats, depending on whether the time signature is 3/4 or 4/4.

If the durations of the notes in a bar add up to more than the right number of beats, the computer will print BAR ERROR. It will still play the tune, though.

```
TIME 3/4
--------------1
 1   C-1   1
 2   D-1   1
 3   E-1   2
BAR ERROR
--------------2
```

You can get rid of a BAR ERROR by changing the durations until they add up to the first number in the time signature.

The computer numbers the notes as you type them in. You can use a maximum of 1,000 notes. Press RETURN when you have finished and the computer will list what you have written.

Repeats

You can repeat all or part of your tune by pressing **Z**.

-)Z REPEATS

You have three options.

```
1.ADD REPEAT
FROM BAR NUMBER?1
TO BAR NUMBER?2

TIME 4/4
--------------1
RPB
 1   C-2   2
 2   D-2   2
RPE
--------------2
 3   E-2   2
2.REMOVE REPEAT
STARTING AT BAR NUMBER?1
3.REPEAT FROM BEGINNING
```

Repeat begin
Repeat end

You have to tell the computer the bars at which you want the repeat to begin and end. You can use up to three repeats.

The computer will play the notes:
C D C D E

To remove both repeat signs, you tell the computer the bar at which the repeat begins.

Repeat From Beginning (RFB) makes the computer play your tune again from the beginning. It will only do this once. Here it will play
C D C D E F C D C D E F G

To remove the RFB, select option 3 and type a 0.

```
--------------1
RPB
 1   C-2   2
 2   D-2   2
RPE
--------------2
 3   E-2   2
 4   F-2   2
RFB
--------------3
 5   G-2   2
```

Editing your tune

Once your tune is stored in the computer, you can edit it using the commands below. If you list the part of the tune which you want to edit and press RETURN, you can see the notes you are editing.

-)N NEW NOTE

This is a way of changing notes. You type in the number of the note you want to change, press RETURN, and then the pitch and duration of the new note. Press RETURN when you have finished.

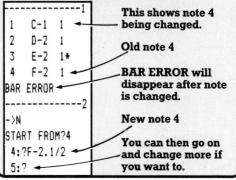

```
--------------1
 1   C-1   1
 2   D-2   1
 3   E-2   1*
 4   F-2   1
BAR ERROR
--------------2
-)N
START FROM?4
4:?F-2.1/2
5:?
```

This shows note 4 being changed.

Old note 4

BAR ERROR will disappear after note is changed.

New note 4

You can then go on and change more if you want to.

-)I INSERT

```
--------------2
 8   A-1   1
 9   C-1   1
10   D-1   1
--------------3
-)I
NOTE NUMBER?9
9:?D-1.1
```

You will be asked NOTE NUMBER? You should type in the higher of the numbers of the two notes between which you are inserting.

The numbers of all the notes after it will be increased by one.

Note to be inserted.

This means new note will be inserted between 8 and 9.

-)D DELETE

```
14   A-1   1
15   G-1   1
16   B-1   1
17   C-1   1
--------------4
-)D
NOTE NUMBER?15
```

The numbers of the notes after it will be decreased by one.

You can only insert or delete one note at a time.

You type in the number of the note you want to delete.

TABLE OF COMMANDS

S – Preset sound. Choose from five.
T – Tempo. 1 = slow; 15 = fast.
K – Keyboard record ON or OFF.
L – Lists the music.
R – Rhythm ON or OFF and select.
P – Play music and rhythm.
M – Menu of pitches and durations.
C – Clear memory.
N – New note, stores notes in memory.
Z – Repeats.
I – Insert a note.
D – Delete a note.

37

Program listing

This is the listing for the program described on page 36. Some lines need changing or adding for different computers. Find the box for your computer on the next page. Mark the lines in the main listing that need changing to remind you to look at the box when you get to these lines.

```
10 GOSUB 1750:GOSUB 1760:GOSUB 1130
20 PRINT:PRINT "->";:GOSUB 1720:PRINT I$:
   LET C=0
30 FOR I=1 TO 12:IF I$=MID$("ZLIDNPRCMKST",
   I,1) THEN LET C=I
40 NEXT I:IF C=0 THEN GOTO 20
50 ON C GOSUB 100,560,420,490,1030,1220,860,
   1100,330,1480,1670,70
60 GOTO 20
70 PRINT "SET TEMPO: (1 - 15)"
80 INPUT TP:IF TP<1 OR TP>15 THEN GOTO 80
90 LET TP=(0.5+TP/10)/7.5:RETURN
100 GOSUB 1750:PRINT "1.ADD REPEAT":
    PRINT "2.REMOVE REPEAT"
110 PRINT "3.REPEAT FROM BEGINNING":PRINT
120 INPUT C:IF C<1 OR C>3 THEN GOTO 120
130 ON C GOSUB 150,220,270
140 RETURN
150 IF BX=7 THEN RETURN
160 PRINT "FROM BAR NUMBER";:INPUT B:IF B<1
    THEN LET B=1
170 LET N=0:FOR I=1 TO 5 STEP 2:IF B(I,1)=B
    THEN LET N=1
180 NEXT I:IF N<>0 THEN RETURN
190 LET B(BX,1)=B:LET BX=BX+1
200 PRINT "TO BAR NUMBER";:INPUT B:
    IF B<=B(BX-1,1) THEN GOTO 200
210 LET B(BX,1)=B:LET BX=BX+1:GOSUB 290:RETURN
220 PRINT "STARTING AT BAR NUMBER";:INPUT B
230 LET N=0:FOR I=1 TO BX-1:IF B(I,1)=B
    THEN LET N=I
240 NEXT I:IF N=0 THEN RETURN
250 LET B(N,1)=1000:LET B(N+1,1)=1000
260 GOSUB 290:RETURN
270 PRINT "AT BAR NUMBER";:INPUT RB:IF RB<0
    THEN LET RB=0
280 RETURN
290 FOR I=1 TO 6:LET L=2000
300 FOR J=I TO 7:IF B(J,1)<L THEN LET L=B(J,1):
    LET N=J
310 NEXT J:LET T=B(I,1):LET B(I,1)=B(N,1):
    LET B(N,1)=T
320 NEXT I:RETURN
330 GOSUB 1750:PRINT:PRINT "PITCHES:"
340 LET C=1:FOR I=1 TO 26
350 PRINT N$(I);" ";:IF C=5 THEN PRINT:LET C=0
360 IF I=12 OR I=25 THEN PRINT:LET C=0
370 LET C=C+1:NEXT I
380 PRINT:PRINT:PRINT "DURATIONS:"
390 PRINT "4*    4   2*    2"
400 PRINT "1*    1":PRINT "1/2* 1/2 1/4* 1/4"
410 RETURN
420 IF TN=MN THEN GOSUB 1710:RETURN
430 PRINT "NOTE NUMBER";:INPUT NP
440 IF NP=0 OR NP>TN THEN RETURN
450 FOR I=TN+1 TO NP STEP -1
460 LET M(I+1,1)=M(I,1):LET M(I+1,2)=M(I,2)
470 NEXT I:GOSUB 930
480 LET TN=TN+1:LET B=NP:GOSUB 570:RETURN
490 IF TN=0 THEN RETURN
500 PRINT "NOTE NUMBER";:INPUT NP
510 IF NP>TN OR NP=0 THEN RETURN
520 FOR I=NP TO TN
530 LET M(I,1)=M(I+1,1):LET M(I,2)=M(I+1,2)
540 NEXT I
550 LET TN=TN-1:LET B=NP:GOSUB 570:RETURN
560 LET B=1:GOSUB 570:RETURN
570 GOSUB 1750:LET LB=0:IF B<1 THEN LET B=1
580 IF TN=0 THEN PRINT "NO NOTES":RETURN
590 LET NB=1:LET BP=1:LET RP=1
600 FOR I=1 TO B:LET LB=LB+D(M(I,2))
610 IF LB>=TB AND I<B THEN LET LB=0:
    LET NB=NB+1:LET BP=I+1
620 IF LB=0 AND B(RP,1)=NB THEN LET RP=RP+1:
    GOTO 620
630 NEXT I:LET B=BP:LET LB=0:GOSUB 760
640 LET I=0
650 IF M(I+B,1)<=0 THEN RETURN
660 PRINT TAB(1);I+B;TAB(5);N$(M(I+B,1));
    TAB(10);D$(M(I+B,2))
670 LET LB=LB+D(M(I+B,2)):IF LB>TB
    THEN PRINT "BAR ERROR"
680 IF LB>=TB THEN GOSUB 790
690 IF LB=0 AND I>6 AND
    I+B<TN THEN GOSUB 740
700 IF I+B<TN AND I$<>CHR$(13) THEN LET I=I+1:
    GOTO 650
710 LET NB=NB+1
720 IF LB<>0 THEN PRINT "BAR ERROR":GOSUB 850
730 RETURN
```

```
740 GOSUB 1720:IF I$=CHR$(13) THEN RETURN
750 GOSUB 1750:GOSUB 760:LET B=B+I:LET I=0:
    RETURN
760 PRINT "TIME ";5-R;"/4":GOSUB 850
770 IF B(RP,1)=NB THEN PRINT "RPB":LET RP=RP+1
780 RETURN
790 LET NB=NB+1:LET LB=0
800 IF B(RP,1)=NB AND B(RP,2)=0 THEN
    PRINT "RPE":LET RP=RP+1
810 IF NB=RB THEN PRINT "RFB"
820 GOSUB 850:IF I>6 THEN RETURN
830 IF B(RP,1)=NB AND B(RP,2)=1 THEN
    PRINT "RPB":LET RP=RP+1
840 RETURN
850 PRINT "--------------";NB:RETURN
860 GOSUB 1750:PRINT "SELECT RHYTHM:"
870 PRINT:PRINT "0 = OFF"
880 IF R=1 THEN PRINT "1 = RHYTHM 1":
    PRINT "2 = RHYTHM 2"
890 IF R=2 THEN PRINT "1 = ON"
900 INPUT C:LET C=INT(ABS(C)):IF (C>1 AND
    R=2) OR (C>2 AND R=1) THEN GOTO 900
910 LET RS=0:IF R=1 AND C=2 THEN LET RS=D(6)
920 LET RF=SGN(C):GOSUB 1750:RETURN
930 LET L$="":PRINT TAB(1);NP;":";:INPUT L$
940 IF L$="" THEN RETURN
950 LET K$=LEFT$(L$,3):LET N=0
960 FOR I=1 TO 26:IF N$(I)=K$ THEN LET N=I
970 NEXT I:IF N=0 THEN PRINT "PITCH ERROR":
    GOTO 930
980 LET M(NP,1)=N
990 LET K$=RIGHT$(L$,LEN(L$)-4):LET N=0
1000 FOR I=1 TO 10:IF D$(I)=K$ THEN LET N=I
1010 NEXT I:IF N=0 THEN PRINT "DURATION ERROR":
     GOTO 930
1020 LET M(NP,2)=N:RETURN
1030 PRINT "START FROM";:INPUT NP:LET PM=NP
1040 IF NP>TN+1 OR NP=0 OR NP>MN THEN RETURN
1050 GOSUB 930
1060 IF L$="" THEN LET B=PM:GOSUB 570:RETURN
1070 IF NP>TN THEN LET TN=NP:LET M(TN+1,1)=0
1080 LET NP=NP+1:IF NP<=MN THEN GOTO 1050
1090 GOSUB 1710:RETURN
1100 PRINT "CLEAR - SURE (Y/N)?"
1110 GOSUB 1720:IF I$="Y" THEN GOSUB 1130
1120 RETURN
1130 FOR I=1 TO MN:LET M(I,1)=0:NEXT I
1140 LET TP=1/7.5:LET RF=0:LET TN=0:LET BX=1:
     LET RB=0
1150 FOR I=1 TO 7:LET B(I,1)=1000
1160 LET B(I,2)=I-2*INT(I/2):NEXT I
1170 LET C=1:GOSUB 1690
1180 PRINT "SELECT TIME:"
1190 PRINT "1 = 4/4":PRINT "2 = 3/4"
1200 INPUT R:IF R<>1 AND R<>2 THEN GOTO 1200
1210 LET TB=D(1+R):LET DR=D(5-R):LET RS=0:
     GOSUB 1750:RETURN
1220 LET NR=RS:LET NM=0:LET BB=RB:GOSUB 1450
1230 TIME=0
1240 LET T=TIME*TP
1250 IF NM<T THEN GOSUB 1310
1260 IF NR<T AND RF=1 THEN GOSUB 1290
1270 IF INKEY$="" THEN GOTO 1240
1280 RETURN
1290 rhythm sound
1300 LET NR=NR+DR:RETURN
1310 IF M(PM,1)=0 THEN RETURN
1320 IF M(PM,1)=26 THEN GOTO 1340
1330 melody sound
1340 LET NM=NM+D(M(PM,2))
1350 LET LB=LB+D(M(PM,2))
1360 LET PM=PM+1
1370 IF LB>=TB THEN GOSUB 1400
1380 IF NB=BB THEN GOSUB 1450:LET BB=0
1390 RETURN
1400 LET LB=0:LET NB=NB+1
1410 IF B(RP,1)<>NB THEN RETURN
1420 IF B(RP,2)=0 THEN LET PM=PP:LET NB=ZB
1430 IF B(RP,2)=1 THEN LET PP=PM:LET ZB=NB
1440 LET RP=RP+1:RETURN
1450 LET PM=1:LET NB=1:LET PP=1:LET LB=0:
     LET ZB=1:LET RP=1
1460 IF B(1,1)=1 THEN LET RP=2
1470 RETURN
1480 LET OC=0:GOSUB 1750:PRINT:
     PRINT "KEYBOARD:"
1490 PRINT "RECORD?":PRINT "1 = ON":
     PRINT "0 = OFF"
1500 INPUT C:LET C=ABS(SGN(C))
1510 IF C=0 THEN LET PM=0:GOTO 1540
1520 PRINT "START FROM ";:INPUT PM:IF PM<1 OR
     PM>TN+1 OR PM>MN THEN GOTO 1520
1530 LET PM=PM-1
1540 LET N=0:GOSUB 1720
1550 FOR I=1 TO 14:IF I$=X$(I) THEN LET N=I:
     LET I=14
```

There is more program over the page.

```
1560 NEXT I:IF N=0 THEN GOTO 1620
1570 IF N=14 THEN LET N=26:GOTO 1600
1580 LET N=N+12*OC
1590 keyboard sound
1600 PRINT N$(N);" ";
1610 IF C=1 THEN LET PM=PM+1:LET M(PM,1)=N:
     LET M(PM,2)=6
1620 IF I$="P" THEN LET OC=1-OC
1630 IF I$<>CHR$(13) AND PM<MN THEN GOTO 1540
1640 IF PM>TN THEN LET TN=PM
1650 IF PM=MN THEN PRINT:GOSUB 1710
1660 PRINT:RETURN
1670 GOSUB 1750:PRINT:PRINT "SELECT PRESET
     (1-5)"
1680 INPUT C:IF C<1 OR C>5 THEN GOTO 1670
1690 ON C GOSUB 1860,1870,1880,1890,1900
1700 RETURN
1710 PRINT "OUT OF SPACE":RETURN
1720 LET I$=INKEY$
1730 IF I$="" THEN GOTO 1720
1740 RETURN
1750 CLS:RETURN
1760 LET MN=100
1770 DIM N$(26),P(25),D$(10),D(10)
1780 DIM M(MN+1,2),X$(14),B(7,2)
1790 FOR I=1 TO 26:READ N$(I):NEXT I
1800 FOR I=1 TO 10:READ D$(I):NEXT I
1810 FOR I=1 TO 10:READ D(I):NEXT I
1820 FOR I=1 TO 13:READ X$(I):NEXT I:
     LET X$(14)=" "       ← Leave a
                            space here.
1830 set pitch values
1840 sound set up
1850 RETURN
1860 preset 1
1870 preset 2
1880 preset 3
1890 preset 4
1900 preset 5
1910 DATA "C-1","C#1","D-1","D#1","E-1",
     "F-1","F#1","G-1","G#1","A-1","A#1"
1920 DATA "B-1","C-2","C#2","D-2","D#2",
     "E-2","F-2","F#2","G-2","G#2","A-2"
1930 DATA "A#2","B-2","C-3","RST"
1940 DATA "4*","4","2*","2","1*","1",
     "1/2*","1/2","1/4*","1/4"
1950 DATA 48,32,24,16,12,8,6,4,3,2
1960 DATA "Q","2","W","3","E","R","5","T",
     "6","Y","7","U","I"
```

Program conversions

Here are boxes with conversions for each type of computer on which the program will run. Substitute the lines in the boxes for those in the main listing. Do not forget to add or leave out lines where indicated, too.

Commodore 64

```
55 POKE S+11,W
1230 TI$="000000"
1240 LET T=TI*TP*1.7
1270 GET I$:IF I$="" THEN GOTO 1240
1290 POKE S+4,128:POKE S+4,129
1310 IF M(PM,1)=0 THEN POKE S+11,W:RETURN
1320 IF M(PM,1)=26 THEN POKE S+11,W:GOTO 1340
1330 POKE S+7,P(M(PM,1),2):POKE S+8,
     P(M(PM,1),1):POKE S+11,W:POKE S+11,W+1
1590 POKE S+7,P(N,2):POKE S+8,P(N,1):
     POKE S+11,W:POKE S+11,W+1
1720 GET I$
1750 PRINT CHR$(147):RETURN
1770 DIM N$(26),P(25,2),D$(10),D(10)
1830 FOR I=1 TO 25:F=2025*2^(I/12):P(I,1)=
     INT(F/256):P(I,2)=F-256*P(I,1):NEXT I
1840 S=54272:FOR I=0 TO 24:POKE S+I,0:NEXT I
1850 POKE S+24,15:POKE S+1,160:POKE S+5,24:
     RETURN
1860 W=32:POKE S+12,9:POKE S+13,0:RETURN
1870 W=32:POKE S+12,88:POKE S+13,89:RETURN
1880 W=16:POKE S+12,9:POKE S+13,9:RETURN
1890 W=64:POKE S+10,8:POKE S+12,9:
     POKE S+13,0:RETURN
1900 W=64:POKE S+10,1:POKE S+12,92:
     POKE S+13,160:RETURN
```

MSX

```
Leave out lines 1860 to 1900
1240 LET T=TIME*TP*2
1245 SOUND 9,0
1290 SOUND 9,15
1330 SOUND 0,P(M(PM,1),2):SOUND 1,P(M(PM,1),
     1):SOUND 13,W:SOUND 12,40/(M(PM,2))/TP
1590 SOUND 0,P(N,2):SOUND 1,P(N,1):
     SOUND 13,W:SOUND 12,20
1690 RETURN
1770 DIM N$(26),P(25,2),D$(10),D(10)
1830 FOR I=1 TO 25:X=450/(2^(I/12)):P(I,1)=
     INT(X/256):P(I,2)=X-256*P(I,1):NEXT I
1840 SOUND 8,16:SOUND 7,42:SOUND 6,15:W=1
```

BBC

```
1270 IF INKEY$(0)="" THEN GOTO 1240
1290 SOUND &0010,2,5,10
1330 SOUND &0011,1,P(M(PM,1)),
     D(M(PM,2))/TP/5
1590 SOUND &0011,1,P(N),10
1720 I$=INKEY$(0)
1830 FOR I=1 TO 25:P(I)=1+4*I:NEXT I
1840 ENVELOPE 2,1,0,0,0,0,0,0,126,-8,0,-1,
     126,0
1860 ENVELOPE 1,1,0,0,0,0,0,0,126,-8,0,-1,
     126,0:RETURN
1870 ENVELOPE 1,1,0,0,0,0,0,0,126,-2,0,-1,
     126,0:RETURN
1880 ENVELOPE 1,1,0,0,0,0,0,0,32,0,-4,-1,
     126,126:RETURN
1890 ENVELOPE 1,2,-1,1,-1,1,2,1,32,0,-4,-1,
     126,126:RETURN
1900 ENVELOPE 1,1,0,0,0,0,0,0,63,-4,-2,-1,
     126,100:RETURN
```

Electron

Use the conversion lines for the BBC, in the box on the left, plus those below.

```
1290 REM
1330 SOUND &0011,1,P(M(PM,1)),D(M(PM,2))/TP/5
1830 FOR I=1 TO 25:P(I)=4*I:NEXT I
1840 REM
1860 ENVELOPE 1,1,0,0,0,0,0,0,0,0,0,0,0,0:RETURN
1870 ENVELOPE 1,1,-1,1,-1,1,2,1,0,0,0,0,0,0:RETURN
1880 ENVELOPE 1,3,-1,1,-1,1,2,1,0,0,0,0,0,0:RETURN
1890 ENVELOPE 1,1,-4,8,-4,1,1,1,0,0,0,0,0,0:RETURN
1900 ENVELOPE 1,4,-4,8,-4,1,1,1,0,0,0,0,0,0:RETURN
```

You cannot use rhythms on the Electron.

There are no rhythms or presets on the Spectrum.

VIC 20

Use the conversion lines for the Commodore 64 (on the previous page), plus those below. If a line appears in both boxes, use the conversion in this one. You need a memory expansion of at least 8K to run this program.

```
Leave out lines 1860, 1870, 1880, 1890 and 1900
55 POKE 36878,0:POKE 36877,0:POKE 36875,0
1235 C=0:POKE 36878,0
1255 V=ABS(V-DV):POKE 36878,V
1265 C=C+1:IF C>1 THEN C=0:POKE 36877,0
1290 POKE 36877,230:POKE 36878,15:C=0
1310 IF M(PM,1)=0 THEN POKE 36875,0:RETURN
1320 IF M(PM,1)=26 THEN POKE 36875,0:GOTO 1340
1330 POKE 36875,P(M(PM,1)):V=15
1355 DV=84/D(M(PM,2))*TP
1590 POKE 36875,P(N):POKE 36878,15
1690 RETURN
1725 POKE 36878,PEEK(36878)-SGN(PEEK(36878))
1770 DIM N$(26),P(25),D$(10),D(10)
1830 FOR I=1 TO 25:P(I)=INT(255.5-127.23/
     (2^(I/12))):NEXT I
1840 POKE 36878,0
1850 RETURN
```

Spectrum

Remember to press CAPS LOCK before typing in or running the program.

```
Leave out lines  1230, 1240, 1260, 1290, 1300,
1340, 1690, 1840 and 1860 to 1900
25 POKE 23692,255
30 FOR I=1 TO 12:IF "ZLIDNPRCMKST"(I)=I$ THEN
   LET C=I
50 GOSUB 100*(C=1)+560*(C=2)+420*(C=3)+490*(C=4)
   +1030*(C=5)+1220*(C=6)+860*(C=7)+1100*(C=8)
   +330*(C=9)+1480*(C=10)+1670*(C=11)+70*(C=12)
130 GOSUB 150*(C=1)+220*(C=2)+270*(C=3)
165 PRINT B
205 PRINT B
225 PRINT B
935 POKE 23692,255
950 PRINT L$:LET K$=L$( TO 3):LET N=0
990 LET K$=L$(5 TO )+"    ":LET K$=K$( TO 4):
    LET N=0
1250 GOSUB 1310
1320 IF M(PM,1)=26 THEN FOR T=1 TO
     D(M(PM,2))*.6/TP:NEXT T:GOTO 1350
1330 BEEP D(M(PM,2))/100/TP,P(M(PM,1))
1525 PRINT PM:PAUSE 20
1590 BEEP 0.2,P(N)
1770 DIM N$(26,3):DIM P(25):DIM D$(10,4):
     DIM D(10)
1780 DIM M(MN+1,2):DIM X$(14):DIM B(7,2)
1830 FOR I=1 TO 25:LET P(I)=I-1:NEXT I
```

← *Leave four spaces here.*

You cannot use presets with the VIC 20 or MSX.

Buyer's guide

On the next four pages you can find out about things that you can buy to enable you to write, play or store electronic music.

On these two pages there is a chart with a list of portable keyboards. It tells you what features they have, as described in this book. There is a key at the bottom of the page to explain the symbols used in the chart. Over the page are music software and hardware for different computers.

All the sections begin with the cheapest item and finish with the most expensive, costing about three times as much as the average home computer.

Keyboards	Keys	Presets	Rhythms	Features
Casio PT-1	29 mk	4	10	sfc, aut
Casio PT-80	32 mk	8	12	sfc, aut, car
Casio MT-36	44 mk	6	4	sfc, aut
Yamaha PS200	37 mk	7	8	sfc, aut, sus, vib
Bontempi HT313	25 mk	6	6	sfc, aut, sus, vib, 5 music games
Bontempi HB404	40 mk	6	6	sfc, aut, sus, vib
Casio MT100	49 mk	20	12	sfc, aut, sus, vib, rev
Yamaha PCS30	32 mk	6	6	sfc, aut, playcard system 3 demonstration songs
Yamaha PSS450	49 mk	12	12	sfc, aut, sus, st
SIEL MK370	37 fk	8	8	sfc, aut, sus, MIDI demonstration song
Bontempi HB414	40 fk	6	8	sfc, aut, sus, vib
Yamaha PS400	44 mk	10	10	sfc, aut, sus
Bontempi HB424	49 fk	6	8	sfc, aut, sus, vib
EKO EM10	49 fk	10	12	sfc, aut, sus, tr
SIEL MK490	49 fk	10	10	sfc, aut, sus, tr, seq, MIDI
Casio MT-400V	49 mk	20	12	sfc, aut, sus, st, filter
Casio MT-85	49 fk	12	12	sfc, aut, sus, car
Casio MT-800	49 fk	12	12	sfc, aut, sus, vib, st, car
EKO EM12	61 fk	10	12	sfc, aut, sus, tr, st
Bontempi HB444	49 fk	6	6	sfc, aut, sus, vib

Keyboards	Keys	Presets	Rhythms	Features
SIEL MK610	61 fk	12	12	sfc, aut, sus, tr, seq, st, PCM, MIDI
Casio CT-430	49 fk	20	12	sfc, aut, sus, vib, rev, st, PCM
Casio CK-500	49 mk	12	12	sfc, aut, sus, vib, rev tape/radio socket
Yamaha PCS500	49 fk	10	10	sfc, aut, sus, st, playcard
Hohner P120N	49 fk	16	12	sfc, aut, sus, vib, spc
Bontempi HB535	49 fk	10	8	sfc, aut, sus, vib
Yamaha MK100	49 mk	12	19	sfc, aut, sus, tr, ch, programmable
Lowrey V-60	49 fk	8	8	sfc, aut, sus, ch, AOC
Casio CT-610	61 fk	20	12	sfc, aut, sus, st
Casio CT-810	49 fk	12	12	sfc, aut, sus, st, car
Viscount VS220	61 mk	12	10	sfc, aut, sus, vib
Technics K-150	49 fk	8	8	sfc, aut, sus, ch, spc, car
JVC KB500B	49 fk	10	10	sfc, aut, sus, st, spc
SIEL MK900	61 fk	20	10	sfc, aut, sus, tr, seq, st, MIDI programmable (manual) rhythms
Bontempi HP555	49 fk	16	16	sfc, aut, sus, vib
Lowrey V-101	49 fk	10	10	sfc, aut, sus, st, ch, AOC tremolo
Yamaha PS35	49 fk	12	16	sfc, aut, sus, st, ch, tr, seq
Technics K-250	49 fk	16	12	sfc, aut, sus, st, spc, PCM

Key to symbols

mk = mini keys

fk = full size keys

sfc = single finger chords

aut = autorhythm/bass

sus = sustain

vib = vibrato

rev = reverb (echo effect)

tr = transpose

seq = sequencer (music store)

st = stereo

ch = chorus, similar to detune

spc = special chord playing facility

car = cartridge to store music

PCM = Pulse Code Modulation

MIDI = MIDI either built in or containing sockets for separate unit

AOC = Automatic organ sounds

Music hardware and software packages

Here is a selection of music packages listed in order of cost, with the cheapest first. New packages are becoming available all the time. Look in computer and music magazines and shops to find out the latest ones.

The packages may have other features not covered by this book.

COMMODORE 64

Music software

ACTIVISION: *Music Maker.* 16 presets which can be edited and stored. Step time sequencer can store three parts with a maximum of 800 notes. All music can be easily edited. Rhythms and repeats can be added. Menu is in the form of pictures (called icons), cursor is controlled by a joystick. Music can be printed on staves.

ISLAND LOGIC: *The Music System.* (The same as the version for the BBC, with the features below.) 30 presets which can be edited. Sequencer can store three parts with up to 1,000 notes. Each note can make the sound of a different preset. A MIDI unit can be added which can store 3,000 sets of information (e.g. pitch, length, preset and so on), called events.

SUPERSOFT: *Music Masters.* 10 presets which can be edited and stored. 18 preset bass/rhythm accompaniments. Stores three parts in real time. Notes are stored by name (i.e. A to G).

Add-on keyboards with software

COMMODORE: *Music Maker.* Two octave plastic keyboard overlay. Ten presets which can be edited. Stores 256 notes in one part over seven octaves. Rhythm, bass and tempo can be programmed. Music displayed on a stave.

LVL: *Organ master* (synthesis only). Three octave keyboard. 15 presets of which four are changeable.

SIEL: *CMK49* (synthesis only). Five octave keyboard. 40 presets, can store 99 polyphonic and monophonic sounds. Good editing facilities.

SIEL: *Sound Buggy.* Sound box which can be used with overlay keyboard or CMK49 (above). Auto-accompaniment rhythms, bass, arpeggios and chords, plus sequencer.

AUTOGRAPHICS: *Microsound.* 49 note keyboard. Two sliding controls can be added to make it easier to edit sounds. Stores three parts, maximum of 200 notes in each.

AUTOGRAPHICS: *Digital Music System.* Samples maximum of ten seconds. Waveform of sample appears on screen. Sections can be reversed, deleted, looped and mixed with others. Number of software packages. Can be linked through MIDI.

ZX SPECTRUM

Music software

SINCLAIR RESEARCH: *Music Master.* (Sequencing only). Stores up to 1,000 notes in step and real time. Comes with 17 key paper keyboard overlay. Prints music.

Music add-on units

DK'TRONICS: *3 Channel Sound Synthesizer* (synthesizer chip called AY-3-8912). Comes with software called Music Designer. Stores three tunes, each one with three parts. Each part can have up to 256 notes. Notes entered using a joystick. Easy editing.

RICOLL: *Action Replay.* Samples up to 7.8 seconds. Reverse, echo, loop, chorus, music. Software allows it to draw sound waves on the screen.

DATEL: *Digital Sound Sampler.* Samples up to 4 seconds. Effects similar to Action Replay (above) with software. Stores up to 1,000 notes.

MSX

Music Computer

YAHAMA: *CX5M.* See page 20 for details.

BBC

Music software

MUSICSOFT: *The Synth.* 11 presets. Stores four different parts in real time with a maximum of 3,000 notes.

ISLAND LOGIC: *The Music System.* 30 presets which can be edited. Stores four parts, which cannot be edited, in step or real time over four octaves. Prints out music.

Music add-on units

ACORN/HYBRID TECHNOLOGY: *Music 500.* Sound box uses special language to sequence 16 different tunes and control synthesis. Separate keyboard can be connected, made by ATPL.

CLEF MUSIC: *Digital CMS.* Five octave, touch sensitive keyboard. 32 presets. Stores eight parts in real time, which cannot be edited, with a maximum of 375 notes.

MIDI unit/software packages

These are listed with the hardware first and the software second. Some MIDI units have more than one OUT socket. This enables them to link together more than one instrument which does not have a THRU socket.

    The computers with which they work are shown in brackets. The packages may have other features not covered in this book.

XRI SYSTEMS: *Micon Interface* (ZX Spectrum). IN, OUT×2, sync*.
Software: 1. *Step Time Sequencer.* Eight parts, full editing and programmable rhythms. 2. *Real Time Sequencer.* Stores eight different parts.

SIEL: *MCI* (Commodore 64, BBC, ZX Spectrum). IN, OUT×2, THRU.
Software (Commodore 64): 1. *Composer/Arranger.* Six separate step time sequencing channels with 1,533 steps in each one. Full editing. 2. *16 Track Sequencer.* 16 polyphonic, real time channels. Stores touch sensitive information. 3. *Keyboard Multitracking.* Allows any combination of MIDI keyboards to be controlled from computer.
Software (BBC): *Composer/Arranger.* Step time sequencer. 6 monophonic channels with 1,018 steps in each. Full editing.
Software (ZX Spectrum): *Live Sequencer.* Stores one track of monophonic music with touch sensitive dynamics.

JMS: *MIDI interface* (Commodore 64, ZX Spectrum). Same sockets as SIEL *MCI.*

Software (Commodore 64): 1. *Step Time Sequencer.* 2. *12 Track Recording Studio.* Sequences twelve different parts in real time.

Software (ZX Spectrum): 1. *Live Sequencer.* Stores in real time. 2. *8 Track Composer.* Stores 8,000 events (notes and information about them).

EMR: *MIDI Track System* (Commodore 64, BBC, ZX Spectrum, MSX). IN, OUT×2, sync*.
Software (all machines): *Performer.* Eight parts recorded in real time. *Composer.* Step time sequencer. *Notator.* Prints out music from Composer program. *Music Editor.* Allows editing of Performer and access to Composer tracks. *Voice Editor.* Allows control over voices in synthesizers.

JORETH: *AL25* (Commodore 64). IN, OUT×3, sync*.
Software: *Sequencer.* Stores eight parts with maximum of 6,000 events.

PASSPORT: *64 MIDI Interface* (Commodore 64). IN, OUT, drum sync*.
Software: *MIDI/4.* Four different parts stored in real time.

U-MUSIC (London Rockshop): *UMI-2B/UMI-1B* (BBC). IN, OUT×4, sync*.
Software: 3,500 note real/step time sequencer. Full editing, good screen display. Stores 127 short sequences of 64 notes.

45

sync = trigger to start instruments.

Electronic music words

Additive synthesis: Way of making sound by combining waves called **harmonics.**

ADSR: Abbreviation for a four-stage **envelope generator: Attack, Decay, Sustain, Release.**

After-touch: Ability of a keyboard to produce **vibrato** when, after pressing, the finger is kept on the key and more pressure applied.

Amplifier: Part of sound system which strengthens sound signal before it is sent to the speaker.

Amplitude: The height of a wave (indicates volume).

Analogue: Continuously varying signal.

Attack: First stage of **envelope;** time volume or **timbre** takes to reach maximum level.

Bar: Section of music containing number of beats indicated by the **time signature.**

Bass-clef: Sign put at the beginning of a **stave** for **bass parts.**

Bass part: Lowest part, played by instruments like the double bass.

Chord: More than one **note** (often three) played at the same time.

Clef: Sign put at the beginning of a **stave** to show which **notes** each line and space represent (see **bass clef** and **treble clef**).

Click track: A regular beat used to keep time when recording in **real time.**

Crotchet: (Quarter note) **Note** with length of one beat.

Cut-off frequency: The **frequency** at which a **filter** removes **harmonics.**

DCO: Digitally Controlled Oscillator (see **oscillator**).

Decay: Second stage of **envelope;** time it takes for volume or **timbre** to drop from maximum to a set level.

Detuning: Making sound "fatter" by altering the **pitch** of one of a pair of **oscillators.**

Digital: In the form of numbers.

Digitizing: Converting a continuously varying (i.e. **analogue**) signal into a series of numbers.

Eighth note: see **quaver.**

Envelope: Description of how the volume or **timbre** of a sound changes while it is sounding.

Envelope generator: Part of **synthesizer chip** making volume or **timbre envelopes.**

Filter: Part of a **synthesizer chip** which lets certain **frequencies** pass and not others.

Flat: Usually a black note named after the white note on its right.

Frequency: How many times a wave vibrates in one second (indicates **pitch**).

Half note: See **minim.**

Harmonics: Sine waves of various **frequencies** which combine to make sounds.

Harmony: A line of music which fits in with the **tune.**

Hertz (Hz): Measurement of **frequency** (i.e. how many times a wave vibrates in one second).

Interval: Distance between two **notes.**

Key: Scale on which a piece of music is based.

Low frequency oscillator: Oscillator producing low **frequency** waves which are combined with other waves to produce **vibrato, trill** and **tremolo** effects.

Lyrics: The words to a song.

Melody: See tune.

MIDI: Musical Instrument Digital Interface. Links up to 16 electronic instruments and computers, allowing one to control all the others.

Minim: (Half note) **Note** with length of two beats.

Modulation: Mixing waves together to produce different effects.

Monophony: Being able to play only one **note** at a time on a keyboard.

Note: Musical sound with a set **pitch** and length.

Octave: Distance between one **note** and the next with the same letter name.

Oscillator: Part of a **synthesizer chip** which produces basic waves.

Parameter: Adjustable synthesizer setting.

Performance control: Synthesizer control (e.g. joystick) which can alter sound while it is being played.

Pitch: How high or low a **note** is.

Polyphony: Being able to play more than one **note** at a time on a keyboard.

Portable keyboard: Small keyboard, usually with built-in speakers and auto-accompaniment.

Portamento: Sliding from one **note** to another, instead of them sounding separately.

Preset: A type of sound stored in a synthesizer.

Program: Instructions which tell a computer what to do. Usually stored on tape or disk.

Programmable synthesizer: One on which **presets** can be altered and stored.

Pulse width modulation: A type of **modulation** where a **square wave** is made rectangular.

Quarter note: See **crotchet.**

Quaver: (Eighth note) **Note** with length of half a beat.

Real time: Way of storing music by playing it "live".

Release: Final stage of **envelope**; time it takes for the volume or **timbre** to die away.

Resonance: Ringing effect caused by increasing the **amplitude** of **harmonics** around the **cut-off frequency** in a **filter.**

Rest: A beat, part of a beat or number of beats where no **note** is being played.

Rhythm part: Part of music played by percussion instruments.

Ring modulation: Modulation producing a bell-like sound.

Sampling: Recording a sound and storing it as a set of numbers.

Sawtooth wave: Basic wave used to make brass sounds.

Scale: Sequence of eight notes with fixed pattern of **tones** and **semitones** between them.

Semibreve: (Whole note) **Note** of four beats duration.

Semitone: Name for the distance between two adjacent notes, usually one white, one black (e.g. C and C#).

Sequencer: A machine on which music can be stored and played.

Sharp: Usually a black note named after the white note on its left.

Sine wave: Wave which represents a pure note; shape of a **harmonic.**

Software: See **program.**

Split keyboard: Keyboard on which different groups or sections of notes can produce different types of sounds.

Square wave: Basic wave used to make clarinet-type sounds.

Stave: Set of five lines on which music is written.

Step time: Storing music one **note** at a time, telling the synthesizer or computer its **pitch** and length.

Subtractive synthesis: Making sound by removing **harmonics** from basic waves.

Sustain: Last but one stage of an **envelope** – level at which **note** remains until the key is released.

Synchronization: Modulation producing a harsh metallic sound.

Synthesis: Making sounds using electronic circuitry.

Synthesizer chip: Main part of the electronic circuitry which produces sound signals.

Tempo: Speed of music measured in beats per second.

Timbre: Quality of a sound which makes it different from others.

Time signature: Numbers at the beginning of written music which indicate how many beats in a **bar.**

Tone: Distance of two **semitones** (e.g. between C and D).

Touch sensitivity: Keyboard which responds to how hard or quickly each key is pressed.

Transposing: Raising or lowering the **pitch** of a **note** or **key** of a piece of music.

Treble clef: Sign at the beginning of the music for upper half of the keyboard.

Tremolo: Rapid alternating of the volume of a **note** between two levels.

Triangular wave: Basic wave used for flute-like sounds.

Trigger: An electrical signal which can be sent through **MIDI** to start an electronic instrument, such as a rhythm machine.

Trill: Rapid switching between two **notes.**

Tune: (Melody) The main musical part to which the **lyrics** are sung.

VCA: Voltage Controlled Amplifier. (See **amplifier.**)

VCF: Voltage Controlled Filter. (See **filter.**)

VCO: Voltage Controlled Oscillator. (See **oscillator**).

Vibrato: Sound which slides rapidly and repeatedly between two **pitches.**

Wavelength: Distance between two peaks of a wave.

White noise: Random wave which produces a hiss.

Whole note: See **semibrave.**

Index

First published in 1985 by Usborne Publishing Ltd., 20 Garrick Street, London, WC2E 9BJ, England.
© 1985 Usborne Publishing
The name Usborne and the device   are Trade Marks of Usborne Publishing Ltd.